THE THRONE OF ADULIS

EMBLEMS OF ANTIQUITY

Font of Life

Ambrose, Augustine, and the Mystery of Baptism

GARRY WILLS

Medusa's Gaze

The Extraordinary Journey of the Tazza Farnese

MARINA BELOZERSKAYA

The Throne of Adulis

Red Sea Wars on the Eve of Islam

G. W. BOWERSOCK

The Throne *of* Adulis

Red Sea Wars on the Eve of Islam

G. W. BOWERSOCK

OXFORD
UNIVERSITY PRESS

OXFORD
UNIVERSITY PRESS

Oxford University Press is a department of the University of Oxford.
It furthers the University's objective of excellence in research,
scholarship, and education by publishing worldwide.

Oxford New York
Auckland Cape Town Dar es Salaam Hong Kong Karachi
Kuala Lumpur Madrid Melbourne Mexico City Nairobi
New Delhi Shanghai Taipei Toronto

With offices in
Argentina Austria Brazil Chile Czech Republic France Greece
Guatemala Hungary Italy Japan Poland Portugal Singapore
South Korea Switzerland Thailand Turkey Ukraine Vietnam

Published in the United States of America by
Oxford University Press
198 Madison Avenue, New York, NY 10016

Library of Congress Cataloging-in-Publication Data
Bowersock, G. W. (Glen Warren), 1936–
The Throne of Adulis : Red Sea wars on the eve of Islam / G. W. Bowersock.
p. cm.—(Emblems of antiquity)
Includes bibliographical references and index.
ISBN 978-0-19-973932-5
1. Himyar (Yemen)—History—6th century. 2. Jews—Yemen (Republic)—Himyar—History—
6th century. 3. Arabian Peninsula—History—To 622. 4. Aksum (Kingdom)—History 6th century.
5. Red Sea Region—History—6th century. 6. Judaism—Relations—Christianity—History—
6th century. 7. Christianity and other religions—Judaism—History—6th century. I. Title.
II. Series: Emblems of antiquity.
DS231.B69 2013
939.49—dc23 2012023593

5 7 9 8 6 4

Printed in the United States of America
on acid-free paper

Contents

Maps and Illustrations

Map 1. Late Antique East Africa, map based on William Y. Adams, *Nubia. Corridor to Africa* (Princeton, 1984), p. 384. xxi

Map 2. Late Antique Southwest Arabia, map based on I. Gajda, *Le royaume de Ḥimyar à l'époque monothéiste* (Paris, 2009), p. 139. xxii

Fig. 1. Drawing of the Adulis Throne in Ethiopia as given in three manuscripts of Cosmas Indicopleustes, from W. Wolska-Conus, Cosmas Indicopleustes, *Topographie Chrétienne*, Vol. 1, Sources chrétiennes no. 141 (Paris, 1968), p. 367. 13

Preface

The idea of a short book centered on the inscribed throne at Adulis first occurred to me over thirty years ago when I read an article that A. F. L. Beeston published in the *Bulletin of the School of Oriental and African Studies* 43 (1980), 453–458. His arresting title was "The Authorship of the Adulis Throne." Because I had long recognized that anything from the pen of Freddy Beeston deserved careful attention, I read his article, which touched upon work that I was doing at the time on Roman Arabia, with particular interest. Some ten years before that, Freddy had attended a lecture I gave in Oxford on Roman policy in the Near East, and his conversation was then, as it always was, convivial, instructive, and memorable. We met again occasionally after that, but his work was never far from my desk. Freddy had rightly identified the inscription on the

Adulis Throne as a still unsolved problem. Although he was not concerned with the other, and much earlier, inscription on the stele that lay beside the throne, his reflections on the throne text showed his legendary mastery of South Arabian language and epigraphy.

Like most scholars today, I cannot accept the hypothesis that Freddy advanced, albeit with due caution, as an interpretation of the throne inscription, and at this late date there is no point in trying to engage with it or refute it. His notion that a Ḥimyarite king put up the throne and its inscription cannot now withstand the powerful evidence of the Ethiopic epigraphy at Axum or of the many other thrones for which traces survive. But Freddy saw clearly that the throne at Adulis, which first received widespread attention only when J. W. McCrindle published his English translation of Cosmas Indicopleustes in 1897, could be a fundamental document for understanding the complex wars and religious struggles that played out in the Red Sea area in the three or four centuries before Islam. Freddy's article in 1980 was pathbreaking.

When I published my *Roman Arabia* in 1983, the Jewish kingdom of converted Arabs in Ḥimyar had seemed to me perhaps the most extraordinary of all the nations of the late antique Near East. As this kingdom lay outside the territory of Roman Arabia, I had contemplated a complementary volume entitled *Jewish Arabia*, but at that time it seemed that such a title might bring more misunderstanding than enlightenment. The documentation then was considerably more exiguous than it is now. But with all that we have learned in recent years, the story of the Jews of Ḥimyar, in the context of their relations with Ethiopian Christians across the Red Sea, has become much more accessible. This is what I have attempted to explore by examining the manifold implications of the Adulis Throne from the Ptolemies to Muḥammad.

I have had the good fortune of working with a former Princeton graduate student, George Hatke, who had similarly discovered, entirely on his own, the fascination of the Ḥimyarite–Ethiopian confrontation. I was delighted when he invited me to serve as a reader for his thesis, directed by my friend and colleague Michael Cook. Hatke successfully defended his work in November 2010, and I hope very much that the thesis will be published in the near future. It currently bears the title *Africans in Arabia Felix: Aksumite Relations with Ḥimyar in the Sixth Century C.E.* and will be an invaluable resource for scholars who wish to do further research on this topic.

Finally, some of the issues I have raised in my final chapters in connection with the struggles between Ethiopia and South Arabia overlap the first of three lectures that I delivered in Jerusalem in April 2011 in memory of Menahem Stern. These lectures, *Empires in Collision in Late Antiquity*, carry forward the Byzantine–Persian conflict and the rise of Muḥammad into the seventh century. They examine the Persian capture of Jerusalem in 614 (second lecture) and the collapse of the Persian empire (third lecture). With my head full of this material, I responded with enthusiasm to Stefan Vranka's imaginative idea for a series of volumes on emblematic objects or events in history by reviving the excitement I had felt long before in reading Freddy Beeston's demonstration that the Adulis Throne evoked the whole complex world of Red Sea imperialism and religion. Hence I owe no less to Stefan than to Freddy for making this book happen. It will be obvious to any scholar in the field how much I owe to the pioneering work of Christian

Julien Robin and his colleagues in Paris. The recent growth of South Arabian epigraphy, of which Robin is a master, has provided welcome confirmation of traditions and suppositions that have been discussed for centuries. As so often in the past, I am deeply indebted to Christopher Jones of Harvard, my friend and colleague of more than fifty years, for a critical reading of these pages.

G. W. Bowersock
Princeton, August 2012

Abbreviations

BSOAS *Bulletin of the School of Oriental and African Studies (London).*

BASOR *Bulletin of the American Schools of Oriental Research.*

CAC *Catalogue of the Aksumite Coins in the British Museum, ed. Stuart Munro-Hay (London, 1999).*

CIH *Corpus Inscriptionum Himyariticarum: Corpus Inscriptionum Semiticarum, Pars Quarta inscriptiones himyariticas et sabaeas continens.*

CRAI *Comptes-Rendus de l'Académie des Inscriptions et Belles-Lettres (Paris).*

DAE *Deutsche Aksum-Expedition (Berlin, 1913). Vol. 2, Daniel Krencker, Ältere Denkmäler Nordabessiniens. Vol. 4: Enno Littmann, Sabäische, griechische und altabessinische Inschriften.*

FGH *Die Fragmente der griechischen Historiker (Jacoby).*

FHG *Fragmenta Historicorum Graecorum, ed. C. Müller.*

FHN *Fontes Historiae Nubiorum. Vol. 2: From the Mid-Fifth to the First Century BC, and Vol. 3: From the First to the Sixth Century AD, ed. Tormod Eide, Tomas Hägg, Richard Holton Pierce, László Török (Bergen, 1998).*

JRS *Journal of Roman Studies.*

JSAI *Jerusalem Studies in Arabic and Islam.*

MarAr *Le martyre de Saint Aréthas et de ses compagnons (BHG 166), ed. Marina Detoraki with translation by Joëlle Beaucamp (Paris, 2007).*

RdA *Routes d'Arabie. Archéologie et Histoire du Royaume d'Arabie Saoudite, ed. Ali Ibrahim Al-Ghabban et al., Catalogue de l'exposition au Louvre (Paris, 2010).*

RIE *Recueil des Inscriptions de l'Éthiopie des périodes pré-axoumite et axoumite. Vol. 1. Les documents and Vol. 2 Les planches (Paris, 1991). Vol. 3 Traductions et commentaires. A. Les inscriptions grecques (Paris, 2000).*

SEG *Supplementum Epigraphicum Graecum.*

TAPA *Transactions of the American Philological Association.*

Timeline

246–241 BC	Third Syrian War of Ptolemy III Euergetes
27 BC	Foundation of the Roman Empire under Augustus

All dates below are CE/AD.

ca. 50	Composition of the *Periplus of the Red Sea*
ca. 200–270	First Ethiopian occupation of Ḥimyar
ca. 330–380	Reign of Aezanas at Axum in Ethiopia

ca. 340	Conversion of Aezanas to Christianity
ca. 380	Conversion of Ḥimyar to Judaism
ca. 450	MḤDYS *negus* in Axum, imitator of Constantine
ca. 470	Martyrdom of Azqīr in Ḥimyar
491–518	Anastasius Emperor in Byzantium
502	Embassy of Euphrasius to Kinda
518–527	Justin Emperor in Byzantium
ca. 517–533	Kālēb (Ella Asbeha) *negus* in Axum
522–525	Yūsuf, Jewish king in Ḥimyar
523	Massacre of Christians at Najrān
524	Embassy of Abraham to Naṣrid al Mundhir and Conference of Ramla
ca. 524	Visit of Cosmas Indicopleustes to Adulis
525	Ethiopian Invasion of Arabia and death of Yūsuf
527–565	Justinian Emperor in Byzantium

528	Embassy of Abraham to Kinda
530	Embassy of Nonnosus to Kinda and Axum
531	Embassy of Abraham to Kinda
ca. 527–565	Ethopian Abraha King in Ḥimyar
548	Conference at Mārib
ca. 549	Cosmas writes the *Christian Topography*
552	Abraha's campaign into northern Arabia
ca. 565	Sassanian Persians take control of Ḥimyar
ca. 570	Traditional date for the birth of Muḥammad
602–610	Phocas Emperor at Byzantium
614	Capture of Jerusalem by the Sassanian Persians
622	*Hijra* (migration) of Muḥammad from Mecca to Medina
610–641	Heraclius Emperor at Byzantium

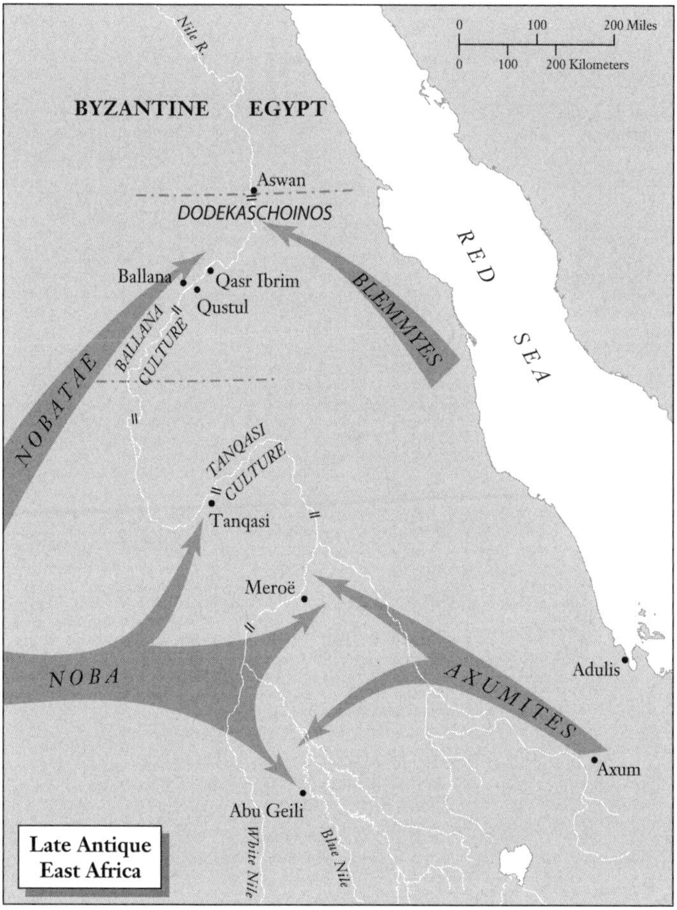

Map 1. Late Antique East Africa, map based on William Y. Adams, *Nubia. Corridor to Africa* (Princeton, 1984), p. 384.

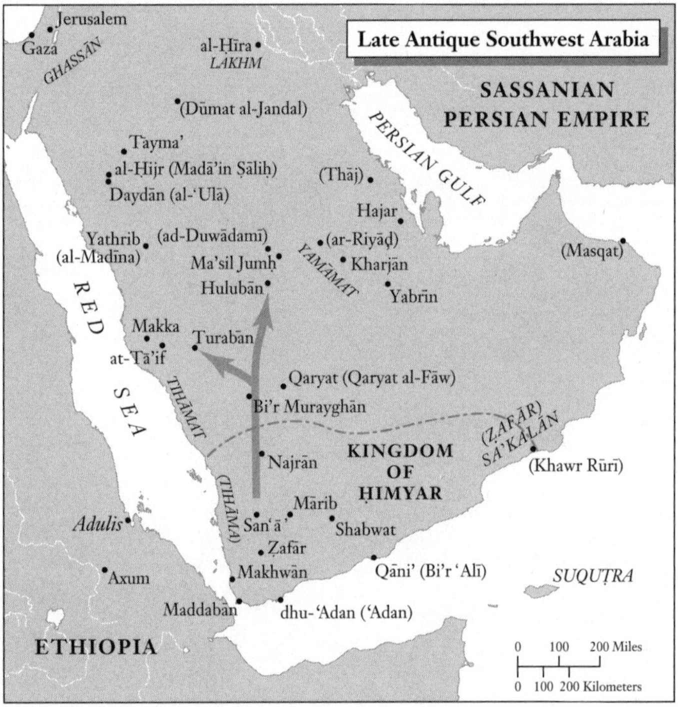

Map 2. Late Antique Southwest Arabia, map based on I. Gajda, *Le royaume de Ḥimyar à l'époque monothéiste* (Paris, 2009), p. 139.

THE THRONE OF ADULIS

PROLOGUE

In the southwestern part of Arabia, known in antiquity as Ḥimyar and corresponding today approximately with Yemen, the local population converted to Judaism at some point in the late fourth century AD, and by about 425 a Jewish kingdom had already taken shape. After that for just over a century its kings ruled, with one significant interruption, over a religious state that was explicitly dedicated to the observance of Judaism and the persecution of its Christian population. The record has survived through many centuries in Arabic historical writings, as well as in Greek and Syriac accounts of martyred Christians. For a long time incredulous historians had been inclined to see little more than a local monotheism overlaid with language and features that had been borrowed from Jews who had settled in the area. It was only toward the end of the last century that enough inscribed stones turned up to prove definitively the veracity of these surprising accounts. We can now say that an entire nation of ethnic Arabs in southwestern Arabia had converted to Judaism and imposed it as the state religion.

This bizarre but militant kingdom in Ḥimyar was eventually overthrown by an invasion of forces from Christian Ethiopia on the other side of the Red Sea. They set sail from East Africa, where they were joined by reinforcements from the Christian emperor in Constantinople. In the territory of Ḥimyar they engaged and destroyed the armies of the Jewish king and finally brought an end to what was arguably the most improbable, yet portentous upheaval in the history of Arabia before Islam. Few scholars, apart from specialists in ancient South Arabia or early Christian Ethiopia, have been aware of these events, but a vigorous and talented team led by Christian Julien Robin in Paris has recently pioneered research on this Yemenite Jewish kingdom.

No one can look at the kingdom of Jewish Arabia without constant reference to its neighbors—the Ethiopians at Axum in East Africa, the Byzantines in Constantinople, the Jews in Jerusalem, the Sassanian Persians in Mesopotamia, and the Arab sheikhs who controlled the great tribes of the desert. Soon after 523 all these powerful interests had to confront a savage pogrom that the Jewish king of the Arabs launched against the Christians in the city of Najrān. The king himself reported in excruciating detail to his Arab and Persian allies about the massacres he had inflicted on all Christians who refused to convert to Judaism. News of his infamous actions rapidly spread across the Middle East. A Christian who happened to be present at a meeting of an Arab sheikh at which the Jewish king reported on his persecution was horrified and immediately sent out letters to inform Christian communities elsewhere. When word of the pogrom reached Axum in Christian Ethiopia, the king who had his capital there seized the opportunity to rally his troops and cross the Red Sea in aid of the Arabian Christians.

Religion was undoubtedly the common denominator for what proved to be widespread international interference in Arabian affairs. But the Ethiopians used their Christian faith to carry out a mission that also favored imperialist designs of their own and, at the same time, supported the Byzantine emperor, for whom a desire to undermine the Persian empire had reinforced his Christian zeal in attacking the Arabian Jews. Both the converts and the Jewish settlers from an earlier era who had been living in Yathrib (the future Medina) profited from Persian sympathy, as did at least one large tribal confederation in the desert. The only losers in these diplomatic and military initiatives were the traditional Arab pagans who survived inside and outside Ḥimyar. They could be found all over, but conspicuously farther north in the peninsula, precisely where, a half-century later, the prophet Muhammad would be born. What became the Ka'ba of Islamic Mecca was reported once to have been a shrine of the pagan deity Hubal.

The Jewish kingdom of Arabia came to an end in 525, when the Ethiopians replaced it with a Christian kingdom of their own, but the legacy of the Ḥimyarite persecution left its traces in the Arabic, Syriac, and Greek traditions. Persian sympathy for the Jews generally continued undiminished, particularly when they themselves managed to expel the Ethiopian overlords of Ḥimyar on the eve of Muhammad's birth, allegedly in 570 or thereabouts. The Persians moved on to capture Jerusalem in 614, where they were welcomed as liberators by the Jewish population. But a little more than two decades later the armies of a new monotheistic faith had surged out of Arabia into Palestine and posed the greatest challenge to their monotheistic predecessors, the Jews and the Christians, that either had ever confronted in the past. In 638 Sophronius, the Christian patriarch of Jerusalem, turned over the city to the Arab caliph ʻUmar.

The extraordinary history of Judaism in Arabia in the Red Sea region provides an indispensable and much neglected background for the rise of Islam as well as the collapse of the Persian empire before the Byzantines. At the heart of this historical drama is a Greek text that was inscribed on a monument that had lain for at least several centuries on the soil of a port city in the territory of the modern state of Eritrea. A Christian merchant saw it in the sixth century and described it with care. It was in the shape of a throne, and because of its location at the town of Adulis it has become known as the Adulis Throne. Trying to understand this monument takes us directly into religious conflicts that occupied the nations on both sides of the Red Sea in late antiquity. These conflicts had deep and ancient roots going back many centuries earlier, as becomes clear from a second inscription that had been cut on a stone that lay alongside the throne. The throne no longer exists at Adulis, but it still offers the best way into the strange story of Jewish Arabia.

1

THE THRONE

In northeast Africa along the coast of Eritrea facing the Red Sea not far from the modern city of Asmara, a deep gulf cuts into the land towards the interior. It provides shelter from the winds in the Red Sea and a measure of security from the islands that lie near its entrance. This gulf, into which run several river valleys from the Ethiopian highlands, was called Annesley Bay in the colonial period as a commemoration of the British traveler George Annesley, who explored the region in the first decade of the nineteenth century. Today it is known as the Gulf of Zula, proudly displaying the name that it had borne, in a slightly different form, two thousand years earlier. In Graeco-Roman antiquity the gulf provided the principal point of access by sea to the southern interior comprising the Ethiopian highlands, and, in late antiquity, the Christian kingdom that had its capital at Axum.

From the sea any journey into the interior and to Axum itself had to begin from the port city of Adulis, which lay just a few kilometers inland from the western shore of the Gulf of Zula. It is the very name of Adulis that passed into that of Zula by way of a deformation as Azulis, which generated its present local toponym Azouli. The etymology of the word Adulis remains a mystery to this day, because it could be either Greek or Semitic, and there is no way of telling which it is. If Greek, the word would imply, from the privative prefix *a-*, an absence of slaves (*douloi*), but such an explanation seems highly implausible. Scholarly efforts to turn the name into a reference to a settlement of former slaves, who, being no longer enslaved, might be said to live in a "slave-less" place, are desperate measures that few have been willing to accept. But if the word is not Greek but Ethiopic, which is a Semitic language, the **ad** element would mean "place," and that seems much more promising. A tribal designation of some kind might follow, and so "place of the Uli or Ule" may be the answer to this puzzle, exactly as Enno Littmann once suggested.[1]

Whatever the etymology, travelers both ancient and modern have noticed the scattered ancient remains a little to the east of Azouli, where Henry Salt identified the site in 1810 and the British first excavated in 1868. The foundations of several buildings, including a church, were discovered there, and subsequent excavations at the site by the Italians and French have turned up structures, coins, and artifacts that point to a relatively late period (2nd to 7th centuries AD) for the extant traces. Some of these pieces have been transferred to the Asmara museum. The church, of which remains are held in the

British Museum, appears to be Byzantine, and another church of comparable date appeared in the Italian work under the Fascists. More recent French excavation at Adulis as well as a British survey reinforces the late date for the surviving remains. The ruins and objects, together with the name of Azouli itself, serve to establish decisively the location of the site.[2] It lay near the confluence of three rivers and stood on the northern bank of one of them, the Haddas river. From antiquity to the present the Haddas served as a major route southwestward into the interior highlands and the territory of Axum.

In ancient literature Adulis appears as early as a famous merchant's manual known as the *Periplus of the Red Sea*. This is a guide to ports for trading vessels operating across the Indian Ocean between the coasts of India and East Africa, and through the notoriously treacherous Bab al Mandab ("Gate of Lamentation") up the Egyptian coast along the Red Sea. The *Periplus* includes detailed information about routes and commercial products in these regions during the middle of the first century AD. This date is now secure thanks to our knowledge of the reign of Malichus II, who is named in the text as king of the Nabataean Arabs in Transjordan. Coins and inscriptions guarantee that his rule encompassed the years 40–70 AD.[3] In describing the East African side of the Red Sea the manual states:

> About 3000 stades beyond Ptolemaïs of the Hunts [a city farther north along the coast] is the legal emporium Adulis. It is on a deep bay extending due south, in front of which lies an island called Oreinê

> that is situated about 200 stades into the farthest part of the bay towards the open sea and on both sides lies parallel to the coast; here at the present time arriving vessels moor because of raids from the mainland. Formerly they used to moor in the deepest part of the bay at the island called Didôros Island, right by this part of the coast; here is a ford crossing to it by which the Barbaroi dwelling roundabout used to overrun the island.[4]

The merchant's description fits reasonably well the topography of Azouli on the Gulf of Zula, and the distance of approximately 3000 stades (300 miles) from Ptolemaïs of the Hunts, which, in all probability, is modern Aqiq, is reasonable. Unfortunately, the account of the offshore islands immediately alongside the gulf is couched in language that is far from perspicuous. Oreinê would appear to correspond with the island Dese at the head of the Gulf, whereas the account of Didôros Island as lying just outside the bay can only be explained if the island, to which the barbarians had access by a ford, has now become absorbed into the mainland through silting. One can only surmount the difficulty of correlating the description with today's geography by postulating such a change in the coastline, and this is what the latest British team has reasonably proposed to solve the problem. One result of failing to recognize this change has been that the merchant's description has impelled some commentators to propose that Adulis actually lay at Massawa in modern Eritrea, with its fine port, some forty miles to the north on the coast—an identification that appeared to be strengthened by the merchant's reference to "numerous small, sandy islands" as one sailed out of the port into the open sea. Certainly the more than two hundred islands of the Dahlak archipelago between Massawa and the entrance into the Gulf of Zula correspond perfectly well with this description.[5] But the ancient remains and the toponymy of the site that Salt identified long ago leave no doubt that his identification was correct.

By contrast, Adulis, though clearly identified as a port city, must have stood, like the present site, a few miles back from the coastal shoreline. Although it lacked any harbor of its own, this fact in no way invalidates its powerful claim to be a port city. It lies today some 7 kilometers from the water rather than the 20 stades (3.3 kilometers) indicated by the merchant manual, but silting can easily account for the difference, and a port town set back from the actual harbor would hardly surprise anyone who knows the relation of Piraeus to Athens or Ostia to Rome. It would be impossible to separate Adulis from the ruins near Azouli. The anonymous author of the *Periplus* was quite correct, however, when he said that it was an eight-day overland journey to the metropolis he called Axômitês, by which he obviously meant Axum. He clearly understood that Adulis was the place from which Axum had access to the sea and, equally, foreigners had access to Axum.

If the town of Adulis was situated, as it evidently was, some distance inland from the gulf coast, it necessarily cannot be imagined as the actual harbor at which maritime traffic with Axum would have anchored. But fortunately we know where that harbor was. It lay where there was a customs station by the name of Gabaza, directly on the coast farther into the southern end of the gulf. This place is mentioned in an account of the martyrdom of the Christian Arab Arethas in the sixth century, where it is explicitly described as an anchorage that was dependent upon Adulis.[6] Hence Gabaza was the actual harbor for Adulis as the port city. Confirmation of this can be found in an extraordinary map of the region (*Fig. 1*) that occurs in the three manuscripts of a work by a sixth-century Christian traveler, Cosmas Indicopleustes, of whom we shall have much to say in the pages that follow. In this map Gabaza shows up, exactly as the Arethas text suggests, near Adulis but deeper into the gulf. The recent British survey team has persuasively identified Gabaza with the Galala Hills south of Adulis and Didôros Island as a hill that coastal change has now permanently attached to the mainland.[7] The name itself, Gabaza, may possibly allude to a minor kingdom that could be inferred from a numismatic reference to a sixth-century king Ella Gabaz.[8] In any case, the form of the name appears to be derived from the verbal root for "protect" or "guard" in Ge'ez (the classical language of ancient Ethiopia). The word Gabaza appears once again, without any allusion to the port, in a late antique Ethiopic inscription that apparently attaches this name to the cathedral at Axum.[9] This would appear to reflect the dependence of the Christian kingdom of Ethiopia on the region that controlled both its trade and its naval activity in the Red Sea. To this the Gulf of Zula provided sole access. It was Axum's window on the Arabian peninsula that lay across the water.

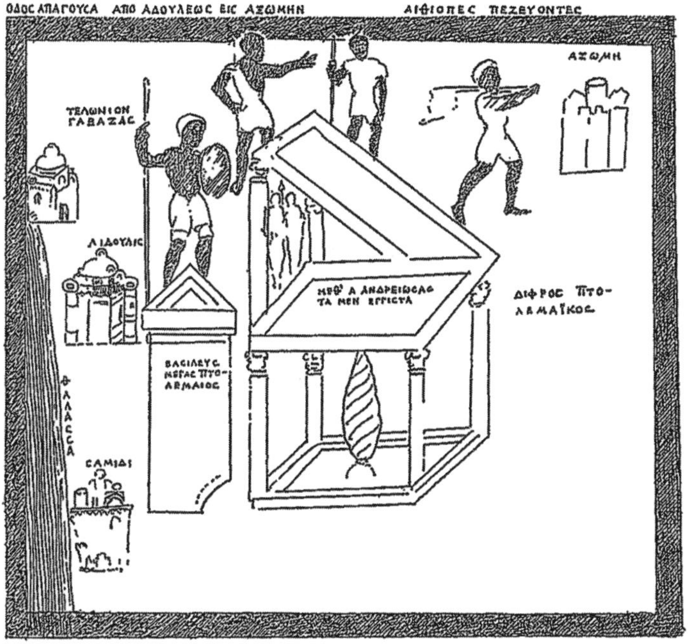

Figure 1. Drawing of the Adulis Throne in its geographical setting, as preserved in three manuscripts of Cosmas Indicopleustes. This drawing is oriented with North at the bottom and South at the top. Hence the northermost part of the Gulf of Zula is located at the bottom, with, going upward to the South, Samidi, Adulis, and the customs station at Gabaza above it. Axum, in the South, appears in the upper right corner with the name given in Greek as Axômê. The artist has reproduced the opening words of the two epigraphical texts that Cosmas cites, and he has erroneously followed Cosmas in thinking all the remains a single Ptolemaic throne. In the top left a Greek label reads, "Road leading from Adulis to Axum," and in the top right the label identifies "Ethiopians on foot." Reproduced from W. Wolska-Conus, Cosmas Indicopleustes, *Topographie Chrétienne,* vol. 1, Sources chrétiennes no. 141 (Paris, 1968), p. 367.

The history of ancient Ethiopia was inextricably bound up with that of South Arabia, including both the land of modern Yemen and the Tihāma coast on the western side of the present Saudi kingdom. The script of classical Ethiopic (Ge'ez), was constructed from the letters that were used for the ancient South Arabian language known as Sabaic, and indeed the very word Ge'ez derives from the Ethiopic verb "to move" or "to migrate." There was a long history of Ethiopian intervention in the Arabian peninsula from the end of the second century AD onwards. Although the Ethiopians were expelled definitively from Arabia in the later third century, their rulers in subsequent epochs, both before and after their conversion to Christianity in the mid-fourth century, did not hesitate to lay claim to the Arabian territories they had formerly held. These lay in southwestern Arabia in a territory that became known as Ḥimyar. Since the Gulf of Zula was indispensable for the launching of expeditions across the Red Sea, the city of Adulis was therefore fundamental in facilitating the ambitions of the Ethiopians to re-establish their control in the Ḥimyarite area of the Arabian peninsula.

Accordingly, it is hardly surprising that Adulis served as a site for the public commemoration of Ethiopia's foreign enterprises. Apart from the ancient remains that have survived for nearly two millennia until modern travelers discovered them, we know, through a literary text that has fortunately been preserved from the sixth century, about one significant monument at Adulis that is not there now. Yet it was clearly emblematic of the achievements and claims of ancient Ethiopia. It symbolized the campaigns against Arabia that Axum launched across the Red Sea in its struggle with a succession of Arab rulers. We know about it from Cosmas Indicopleustes, for whose work the manuscript illustrations of the Gulf of Zula, as mentioned earlier, were created.

Cosmas was a Christian from the so-called Nestorian branch of Christianity that had grown up in the Persian Empire. This is what is sometimes known as the Church of the East. Following Nestorius, the fifth-century patriarch of Constantinople, these Christians differed from Monophysites in emphasizing the human nature of Christ as well as the divine, though accepting the unity of the two (albeit in ways that distinguished them from the Chalcedonian orthodoxy). We do not know Cosmas' real name, although the manuscript tradition has equipped him with a common Christian name derived from the Greek *kosmos* (for world or world order). He undertook to provide for the various Christian nations an annotated geography through a full account of his own international travels across the known Christian world. He did this in a book that bears the title *Christian Topography*. Cosmas had been active in Red Sea trade during the third decade of the sixth century, and it was at this time he went to Adulis.

There he came upon a marble throne that was clearly some kind of commemorative or votive monument—probably both at the same time—and big enough to accommodate a long inscription in Greek.[10] The throne, smaller than a real one that could accommodate a seated human frame but larger than an ornamental collectible, was an object that the Ethiopian king, or *negus* as he was called, had caused to be made and dedicated as a reminder of his victories and conquests. Both before and after the Christianization of the kingdom in the fourth century, dedications of thrones of this kind are mentioned in inscriptions. They were normally offered to the pagan god Maḥrem or his Greek equivalent Ares, just as much later, in the same spirit, they were dedicated to the Christian God, even when the language echoed the traditional forms of pagan dedication. Bases and loose blocks for twenty-six thrones have been found in the old city of Axum, as well as several more thrones in outlying sites.[11]

For the most part, what survives are the stepped blocks of the throne's base, but there are also indications that each throne had side panels and a high back. The German excavators considered that many of the inscribed stone panels found at Axum may once have actually been the sides of thrones. This is far from certain since some of the inscribed stones are simply too big, but others may well have belonged to thrones. The seat itself was called a *manbar* in Ge'ez, from the verb "to sit." By calling it a *diphros*, not a *thronos*, in his Greek narrative, Cosmas appears to have distinguished this somewhat smaller votive throne from a larger one that was big enough to accommodate a king. The word *diphros* is found elsewhere in the Near East as a designation for a small throne,[12] and Cosmas clearly avails himself of this term to designate an Ethiopian votive one.

The drawing (*Fig. 1* above) in the three manuscripts of Cosmas' book, with its depiction of the Gulf of Zula near which Adulis was located, includes a sketch of both the throne and the stele at the site. The drawing of these objects more or less matches Cosmas' description and locates the throne itself in a geographical setting that approximates the topography of the gulf, but, as it is most important to stress, with an orientation in which South is at the top rather than North. The drawing also shows, precisely as Cosmas describes it, an inscription written on the throne as well as, on the back panel, two male figures that presumably represented divinities. On Cosmas' map Adulis is placed close to the coast of the gulf while Gabaza stands, as it should, on the coast itself and is called a customs station (*telônion*). Because of the orientation of the image, with South at the top, Axum appears disconcertingly above Adulis, rather than, as on all modern maps, below it.

The illustration with the Adulis throne in its geographical setting is but one of numerous illustrations in the manuscripts of Cosmas, and it is unclear whether he had any hand in drafting them or whether they were created later by copyists of his text. The oldest of the three manuscripts that contain the drawing of the throne is an uncial Vatican manuscript of the ninth century. The other two, one in the monastery of St. Catherine in Sinai and the other in the Laurentian library in Florence, can be dated to the eleventh century. Whether or not they go back to Cosmas himself, they undoubtedly represent exactly what he describes.[13]

The throne was made of white marble, but not, as Cosmas observes rather pedantically, of marble from the Greek island of Proconnesus. If Cosmas were sufficiently knowledgeable, he may perhaps have been aware that Proconnesian marble had, in fact, been extensively used at Adulis, as modern excavations and surveys have revealed. He tells us that the throne was located at the entrance to the city, on the west side and oriented toward the road to Axum. It had a square base and was supported by four small columns at each of the four corners, as well as by a fifth and thicker column in the middle of the base with a serpentine design. The seat itself was placed on the five columns, with a back standing behind armrests on the right and left sides. The whole was cut out of a single block, measuring a little over three feet in height (2½ cubits). The surface, according to Cosmas, was covered with the Greek inscription.

The Adulis throne, as Cosmas describes it, bears a close resemblance to the thirty odd examples that have been discovered in Ethiopia, but the placement of the seat of the throne on top of pillars at the four corners of the base and one in the middle is altogether unexampled. The sides and back, however, appear consistent with examples that do survive, and the German excavators at Axum have proposed a drawing of the throne in a form comparable to those they discovered.[14] (*Fig. 2*) Since what Cosmas saw may have been made considerably earlier than any of the ancient thrones that the German excavators discovered, it is not impossible that his throne had a more archaic design.

Cosmas goes on to report that behind the throne stood an inscribed stele in black stone, evidently basalt, which was slightly taller than the white marble throne itself. He calls this stele an *eikôn,* which would normally mean an image or statue, but, since the Greek word *stêlê* had, in late antiquity, already taken on the meaning of statue, the old word for statue seems to have replaced it to mean a stele.[15] That this is what Cosmas meant is absolutely clear from the manuscript drawing, in which the stele appears exactly as he describes it with a triangular top "like the letter lambda" (Λ). He wrongly inferred that the inscription on the throne was a continuation of the

Figure 2. A reconstruction of the lost throne and stele at Adulis. This can be no more than a guess, but the inscriptions on the stele and on at least one side panel of the throne are plausible. Adapted from *DAE* p. 66.

inscription on the stele, which was broken at the bottom. No one now doubts that the throne inscription is a totally different document of a different date.[16]

Cosmas reports that the *negus* himself had asked the governor of Adulis to have a copy made of the inscribed texts and sent to him, and the governor entrusted Cosmas with this chore, along with another trader, who, we are told, later became a monk. Fortunately for later generations, Cosmas kept a second copy for himself and decided to include it in his book on Christian topography.

The two Greek texts at Adulis were manifestly far apart in date, but, as Cosmas copied and faithfully reproduced them, they show every sign of being authentic. They have been regularly incorporated into standard epigraphic collections alongside those texts that we know only from stones that survive today. The stele inscription is obviously the earlier one. It is a boastful account of the overseas conquests of Ptolemy III, who ruled the Hellenistic kingdom of Egypt in the third century BC. By contrast, the throne inscription, though lacking its prescript and any identification of the person who caused it to be inscribed, derives without the slightest doubt from an Ethiopian *negus* in the Roman imperial period. His boasts are easily a match for those of Ptolemy and were probably inspired by them. Hence the throne itself, recording the achievements of an Ethiopian ruler in conformity with the indigenous tradition of dedicated and inscribed thrones that are documented in the archaeological record, must postdate the Ptolemaic stele by several centuries at least. Whether the stele was already set up at Adulis when the throne was put there is unclear but seems likely. It is just possible that the dedicant of the throne, or someone else at a later date, had it brought to Adulis, but the obvious imitation of the Ptolemaic inscription in the Ethiopian one makes this most unlikely.

The Adulis throne, therefore, serves as an emblem of ancient Ethiopia in three distinct periods: the reign of Ptolemy III, the reign of the anonymous Ethiopian king under the

Roman Empire, and, finally, the third decade of the sixth century when Cosmas transcribed the texts for a contemporary Christian king in Axum with imperialist ambitions. Cosmas reveals importantly that this king ordered the texts of these boastful inscriptions to be transcribed for him just as he was about to launch a campaign of his own against Ḥimyar on the other side of the Red Sea: "Ellatzbaas [i.e., Ella Asbeha] the king of the Axumites at that time, when he was about to go to war against the Ḥimyarites across the sea, wrote to the governor of Adulis to make an exact copy of what was written on the Ptolemaic throne and the stele, and to send it to him."[17] Cosmas' erroneous inference that the two objects contained parts of the same text obviously led him into the further error of thinking that the throne was Ptolemaic.

The *negus* was manifestly looking for precedents and inspiration for the great expedition that he would soon be launching by ship in the Gulf of Zula not far from Adulis. His overseas campaign against the Ḥimyarites in South Arabia crystalized the irredentist claims of Ethiopia to its former territory in the Arabian peninsula. It brought the Christian Ethiopians into direct conflict with its current rulers, who happened to be, at that time, Arab converts to Judaism. These Arabian Jews had recently carried out a bloody pogrom against the Christians at Najrān in their territory, and this event provided precisely the provocation that the Christian ruler in Ethiopia was looking for. He would now launch an invasion with momentous consequences for the peoples on both sides of the Red Sea, and for nations far beyond them. Byzantium and Persia were ultimately both to join the struggle.

2

A CHRISTIAN TRAVELER IN THE RED SEA

When Cosmas Indicopleustes introduced his account of Adulis and its throne he said that he had gone there as a trader together with other traders from both Alexandria and Elath (at the head of today's Gulf of 'Aqaba): "In Adulis, which is the name for the city of the Ethiopians that lies about two miles from the coast and serves as the port for the people of Axum, where those of us from Alexandria and Elath were engaged in commerce, there is a throne. . . ."[1] This is not the only time when Cosmas identifies himself as a merchant in his *Christian Topography*.[2] His other allusions to personal experiences leave no doubt that he operated in the area of the Red Sea and the Indian Ocean as far as the Persian Gulf and Ceylon, although there is not the slightest reason to believe that he ever went to the Indian subcontinent. The word Indicopleustes, which means "sailor to India," was attached to him in the Middle Ages. Cosmas, as we have seen, is a banal Christian name that was certainly not his real name. It suggests the *kosmos* ("world"), for which the design was of enormous interest to Cosmas.

In fact, the full name Cosmas Indicopleustes does not appear anywhere in the work he actually wrote. The author identifies himself simply as "a Christian," and it was not until the eleventh century that the manuscripts equipped him with the sonorous name by which we know him today, "Cosmas the sailor to India." The reference to India in the epithet *Indicopleustes* can be no more than a reflection of the use of the geographical term "India," both in Cosmas and elsewhere, to refer to a much wider region than the subcontinent that bears that name. Ancient writers applied it freely both to the east coast of Africa and to the southwest corner of the Arabian peninsula. Cosmas reports that in sailing to the Horn of Africa he went to "inner India," and he uses the same expression for the land of Ḥimyar in the Arabian peninsula.[3] He sailed as far as Ceylon, which he correctly designates by its ancient name, Taprobanê, while locating the island as lying in "inner India."[4] The use of "inner" for "more remote" or "outlying" territories in relation to a designated region had a long tradition in ancient geographical writing in both Greek and Semitic languages.[5]

It is clear that Cosmas viewed the base of his operations as lying well to the west of Ceylon in what would have been understood to be a still more remote part of inner India. This can easily be seen from the title of a work ascribed to Palladius, "On the Peoples of India and the Brahmans," in which the author has much to say about the Ethiopians in eastern Africa.[6] Cosmas' world lay in the waters on either side of Arabia, in the Persian Gulf and the Red Sea, as well as in the expanse of the Indian Ocean into which the Red Sea debouches through the Gulf of Aden. This part of the Indian Ocean touched both Somalia in Africa and the south coast of the peninsula from Aden eastwards.

Not surprisingly, Cosmas passed by Socotra on his way between the Red Sea and the Persian Gulf. That island, together with its archipelago, lying off the coast of Yemen to the east of Cape Guardafui, had long been a station for merchants, as can be seen from the reference to it under its ancient name of Dioscourides in the *Periplus of the Red Sea*, which, as we remarked earlier, is now securely anchored to the mid-first century by its reference to the Nabataean king Malichus II (40–70 AD).[7] Cosmas was under the impression that the island had been colonized by the Ptolemies in the Hellenistic period because, although he never put in there himself, he encountered inhabitants of the island when he was in Ethiopia and found that they still spoke Greek.[8] Nevertheless, archaeological remains have failed to indicate any trace of Hellenic culture on Socotra, despite some extraordinary recent discoveries in the cave of Ḥôq on the island. These have revealed other settlements than Greek, including a colony of Palmyrenes in 258 AD, as well as, at an indeterminate date, settlements of Ethiopians and South Arabians. Graffiti in Ethiopic and South Arabian scripts and an inscription on a wooden tablet in Palmyrene Aramaic have been deciphered.[9]

Cosmas was something of an autodidact. He claims to have learned everything he knew from a Christian, Mar Aba, called Patrikios in Greek, with whom he had once studied in Alexandria. That learned cleric ultimately went on to become the archbishop of all the Nestorian communities in Persia. He served in his post from 540 to 552, a time frame that fits perfectly with the apparent period of composition of the *Christian Topography*. Fortunately, this can be determined by Cosmas' assertion that he was asked to furnish the *negus* with copies of the throne inscriptions at Adulis during the visit he made to the site twenty-five years earlier. The imperialist claims of these texts strongly imply that the *negus* was contemplating the great Axumite expedition to Ḥimyar of 525, and this ought to mean that Cosmas was present at Adulis between 523, when the first provocations for war occurred in Arabia, and 525, when the expedition was launched. It is true that Cosmas dates his visit to the "beginning" (*archê*) of the reign of Justin, who ruled as emperor at Constantinople from 518 to 527. But after a quarter-century Cosmas can hardly be expected to be very precise in recalling exactly when Justin came to power. We have to recognize that his work includes references to two solar eclipses that occurred in 547.[10] Hence he could not possibly have been in Adulis before late 522 or early 523, which is the period when the provocations that aroused the Ethiopians began to occur. Accordingly, the various details in Cosmas deliver a date of composition of between 548 and 550, which falls precisely during the episcopate of Cosmas' teacher Patrikios.

As a merchant, Cosmas would naturally have called at the port of Adulis, where he was able to observe and describe the famous throne. Already in the middle of the first century AD this lay along the route of traders in the Red Sea, as the itinerary of the *Periplus of the Red Sea* makes plain. That anonymous work, cited for the location of Adulis in the foregoing chapter, provides a detailed, if not topographically precise account of the town, but its writer was clearly aware of its dependence upon the city of Axum in the highlands to the south. In addition, he alludes to an otherwise unknown king in a broad area that extended southwards another eighty miles or so along the coast from the Gulf of Zula. The king of that entire region in the Horn of Africa, which the *Periplus* calls generally Barbaria, greatly impressed the merchant author of the manual. Although the king's realm probably included the Axumite territory, there is no reason to think that his capital was Axum. Barbaria seems to have been a much more extensive area, probably incorporating modern Djibouti and northern Somalia. The name itself had nothing to do with "barbarians" (the Greek term for non-Greeks) but reflects an indigenous appellation either for the people of Barbaria or conceivably for a divinity such as Barbar who had a temple on the island of Bahrain. The king, we are told, was named Zoskales. Although he is otherwise unattested, we learn from the anonymous merchant that he had a far from superficial knowledge of Greek. His mastery of the written language became evident to the writer in ways we cannot ascertain.[11] But it is worth remembering this early attestation of Greek in the region when we consider the appearance of that language on the Axumite throne inscriptions and on other stones that survive to this day. It is reasonable to assume that Greek was conspicuously used, at least in the upper levels of local administration in East Africa, from the beginning of the Roman Empire and probably before.

Only a decade or two after the *Periplus* was written, the Roman polymath Pliny the Elder also singled out Adulis (*oppidum Adulitarum*) as a great emporium frequented by traders in the region.[12] His subsequent reference in the same passage to a *sinus Abalitu*, in connection with a Diodorus Island, seems not to have been properly understood. This bay (*sinus*) can only indicate the Gulf of Zula. The *Periplus* had explicitly connected it with an island of the same name, and *Abalitu* must therefore be a deformation of *Adulitou*. By his own acknowledgment Pliny was drawing on the scholarly writings of King Juba II of Mauretania for his information: "In this part I have decided to follow . . . King Juba in the volumes he wrote for Gaius Caesar concerning his Arabian expedition."[13] The allusion is to preparation for the campaigns of Augustus' grandson in the East at the end of the first century BC.

Since Juba, who was no less a scholar than a monarch, ruled in North Africa during Augustus' reign and made use of earlier Hellenistic sources for a work that was designed to instruct the young prince, we can safely assume that Adulis was already important as an emporium in the first century BC. This is pertinent for the earlier of the two inscriptions on the throne with its record of the overseas exploits of Ptolemy III. But of course Cosmas, who remains our sole source for these documents, naturally had no sense of the chronological implications of what he had seen and transcribed. His mistaken belief that the two inscribed texts he saw were all part of a single document leaves no doubt about that.

After his career as a merchant Cosmas went on to become, a quarter-century later, the Christian apologist that we know from his book. His travels had clearly instilled in him a profound interest in geography that bore fruit in a work, regrettably lost, in which he had described the entire known world. He refers to it in the prologue to his *Christian Topography* as a work of reference that any reader of the *Topography* should consult. He reports that it encompassed the entire earth and all countries:

> [It is] the volume we wrote for the Christ-loving Constantine, in which the whole earth has been fully described, both this one and what lies beyond the Ocean, as well as all countries: the southern regions from Alexandria to the southern ocean (by which I mean the Nile River and the adjacent regions and peoples of all Egypt and Ethiopia), and the Arabian Gulf with adjacent regions and peoples as far as this same ocean. Equally I include the land between the river and the Gulf, its cities, countries, and peoples.[14]

Assuming his readers would have access to this earlier book, Cosmas devoted himself in his surviving *Topography* to a pious refutation of various cosmological claims advanced by pagans or supposedly misguided Christians, in particular the representation of the universe as a sphere. He had already written a book, now lost like his *Geography*, to describe the movement of the stars and, as he says in his prologue, his objective was "to destroy the error of pagan hypotheses." The ninth book of the *Topography* is also devoted to this subject and presumably resumes what Cosmas had written in his earlier treatise. Most remarkably in the *Topography* Cosmas resumed his spirited defense of the idea that the Jewish tabernacle is an image of the world (*kosmos*). The supposedly apostolic author of the *Epistle to the Hebrews,* Paul or someone else, had declared that Moses, after creating on Sinai the tabernacle that reproduced what he had actually beheld from God, transformed the single tabernacle into two by the interposition of a curtain or veil: one representing the world of mankind and the other the world to come. For Cosmas it was important to establish, from his Christian perspective, that the tabernacle as a whole was a representation of the world.[15]

This meant that for him the universe was a rectangular solid, which he believed to be longer horizontally, from east to west, than it was wide, from north to south. He also believed that the section on the other side of the veil in the Mosaic image of the tabernacle comprehended the heavens, with a cylindrical cap on top. Cosmas considered the entire box that constituted the *kosmos* a kind of house (*oikos*) in the shape of a cube (*kubos*)—despite the differing length and width. The notion of a cube was borrowed from the Septuagint Greek text of Job, for which the original Hebrew offered no equivalent term. As the most knowledgeable modern exegete of the *Topography* has prudently declared, "Cosmas is not rich in geometrical accuracy."[16] Although it is hard to take his idea of the world seriously, particularly for an age in which the spherical representation of the world was commonly accepted, we have to be grateful that Cosmas' preoccupation with this issue led him to write his *Topography*, including all the precious details of his travels. Even if Cosmas' book was by design more a work of theological cosmology than geography, we may be grateful that he felt obliged to illustrate his argument with his geographical knowledge and his practical experience in commerce.

This anonymous person, bearing a banal Christian name that was not his own and obsessed by representations of the world (*kosmos*), could hardly have been more different from the austere merchant-captain who put together the *Periplus of the Red Sea* some five centuries before. For Cosmas Indicopleustes, Adulis was no more than the place where an inscribed throne and an adjacent inscribed stele happened to pique the curiosity of an Ethiopian *negus* who happened to be planning to launch an overseas war. The fact that this *negus* was himself a Christian doubtless moved Cosmas to comply with his request for copies of the inscriptions. On the other hand, he showed no curiosity whatever about the provocations for that Ethiopian war or indeed about the Axumite kingdom itself.

By contrast, the author of the *Periplus* was clearly attentive to the culture he encountered and delivered a precious, if laconic account of it. His observations serve to illuminate the chronological space between the two inscriptions on the Adulis throne. The author's own world was the Roman Empire of the Julio-Claudians, later than the Hellenistic Ptolemies and earlier than the unidentified pagan king at Axum. Adulis, according to the *Periplus*, was a legally recognized trading center, an *emporion nomimon* (legal emporium), on a deep bay extending southwards for about 200 stades (ca. 20 nautical miles) from the open sea. As we have already seen, this is the

Gulf of Zula, the former Annesley Bay. What exactly a "legal emporium" might have been has long been subject to debate, but since the author applies the phrase to only three trading centers out of the thirty-seven that are named in the manual the odds are, as Lionel Casson has argued, that it was a place in which trade was allowed and regulated under the authority of the local ruler and was not simply an open souk or bazaar regulated by some kind of international law.[17] In other words, it was neither a market town legally established as such by the Roman government, nor was it a place that was simply "law-abiding," which would have presumably applied just as well to the thirty-four other ports.

The author of the *Periplus* states clearly that the metropolis of Adulis was Axum, which he calls Axômitês. This certainly implies that what went on there was subject to the authority of its metropolis. Ivory was the chief commodity in Adulis' trade, and the *Periplus* reports that all the ivory "from beyond the Nile" came into Axum and was transported from there to Adulis. The writer goes on to add, "The mass of elephants and rhinoceroses that are slaughtered all inhabit the upland regions, although on rare occasions they are also seen along the shore around Adulis itself."[18] It is therefore not surprising that, as we shall see, the earlier inscription on the site, dating from the reign of Ptolemy III in the third century BC, explicitly refers to elephants in the area.

The vast territory of East Africa, which would appear to have included modern Ethiopia, Eritrea, Djibouti, and Somalia, had been under the rule of the king Zoskales, whose knowledge of the Greek language had so much impressed the author of the *Periplus*. Hence it is not unlikely that this was the ruler who controlled the trade at the "legal emporium" of Adulis in the first century AD because the *Periplus* describes him as "fussy about his possessions and always enlarging them." But, for all that, he was said to have been otherwise a fine person and, of course, steeped in Greek culture. The Hellenic character of this local monarchy in the Julio-Claudian age of the Roman Empire may well have been rooted in prior contact with the Ptolemies, to which the earlier Adulis inscription bears witness. It certainly underlies and explains the continuing use of Greek in the region across the five centuries between the *Periplus* and Cosmas.

Even as the Ethiopic language began to be used in its classical form of Ge'ez, the rulers continued to use Greek to advertise their exploits on the inscriptions they set up alongside parallel texts in Ethiopic. But in the centuries down to Cosmas' day the Ethiopic texts were, on occasion, also inscribed in the alien script of South Arabian (Sabaic), which had to be read from right to left rather than, as in Ethiopic, from left to right. Curiously, it was Greek that served as the link to Ethiopia's more distant past while, at the same time, it provided access to the *lingua franca* of the entire eastern Mediterranean world. Even on the royal coinage of Axum Greek normally appeared together with Ethiopic.

Cosmas' transcription of the Ptolemaic stele therefore carries us back to an era of Greek and ivory, long before the notices of Juba II of Mauretania that were subsequently picked up by the elder Pliny or the visit of the author of the *Periplus* to the port city of Adulis. If Zoskales' realm was as extensive as it seems to have been, the Ethiopian component, with Axum as the metropolis of Adulis, must have been only part of a much larger territory. The rise of the Axumite kings of Ethiopia and their expansion across the Red Sea into the Arabian peninsula would have altered significantly the distribution of power in the lands of East Africa to the south, where Djibouti and Somalia are today. But, as the Ethiopians enlarged their conquests in Africa, they looked increasingly to the north, as well as to the south, and they had good reasons for doing so. A vibrant Nubian civilization centered at Meroë in the territory of the middle Nile posed a major threat to Ethiopia's northern frontier and potentially controlled both the sources of the Nile and access to Egypt, not to mention the ivory that the *Periplus* trader saw at Adulis. This region was destined to threaten and provoke the Ethiopians for several centuries until they brought an end to the Meroitic kingdom.

But the Ptolemaic inscription that Cosmas found and transcribed, although clearly connected in some way with his later text, took his readers much farther back in time than either he or his first readers could possibly have imagined. It evoked a vanished world, the Horn of Africa in the Hellenistic Age, several centuries before Zoskales.

3

PTOLEMY'S ELEPHANTS

Behind the votive throne dedicated by an unnamed Axumite *negus* lay an imposing basalt stele inscribed in Greek, as Cosmas Indicopleustes observed when he went to Adulis in the sixth century AD. The language of the inscription has been universally agreed to be authentic, and so the text transports us back into a remote and unfamiliar epoch in the history of ancient Ethiopia. The subject is the military prowess and overseas conquests of a Hellenistic king, whose name, given with full family details, guarantees that he is Ptolemy III of Egypt, also called Euergetes, who ruled from 246 to 221 BC. The royal house of Egypt took its origins after the death of Alexander the Great from one of his successors called Ptolemy, whose father Lagos supplied the traditional dynastic name of Lagid for all the Ptolemies who ruled Egypt. The inscription is written in the third person but presumably reflects the public image of himself that Ptolemy wished to project, and it boasts of extensive campaigns abroad from Thrace to Mesopotamia. Cosmas' transcription of the text naturally does not provide any indication of the line divisions of the original, but he observed that the stele was broken off at the bottom and thus lacked its concluding part. But, as we have noted earlier, Cosmas was under the mistaken impression that the text inscribed on the stele had been continued into the Greek text that he found written on the throne that stood in front of it.

The Ptolemaic inscription provides a tantalizing glimpse into the extravagant claims of Ptolemy III in foreign policy—claims that need to be understood in the context of his administrative and personal struggles in Egypt. It furnishes details, many of questionable veracity, concerning his conflict in Asia Minor and Syria with the king Seleucus II, whose royal line represented another of the successors of Alexander. Ptolemy's war with Seleucus is generally known as the Third Syrian War. In addition, and most remarkably, the inscription reveals the exploitation of Ethiopia to secure local elephants for military use abroad. Here is what Cosmas read on the basalt stone:

> Great King Ptolemy, son of King Ptolemy and Queen Arsinoe, who are brother and sister gods, themselves the children of King Ptolemy and Queen Berenice, who are savior gods, a descendant on his father's side from Heracles, son of Zeus, and on his mother's side from Dionysus, son of Zeus, having assumed from his father a royal dominion of Egypt,

Libya, Syria, Phoenicia, Cyprus, Lycia, Caria, and the Cyclades islands, led an expedition into Asia with a force of infantry, cavalry, a fleet of ships, and elephants from Troglodytis and Ethiopia. These animals his father and he himself first hunted out from these places and brought to Egypt for use in war. Having become master of all the land west of the Euphrates—Cilicia, Pamphylia, Ionia, the Hellespont, Thrace, and of all the armed forces in those lands as well as Indian elephants, and having brought the monarchs in all those places into subjection to him, he crossed the Euphrates river and subdued Mesopotamia, Babylonia, Susiana, Persis, Media, and all the remaining territory as far as Bactriana. He recovered all the holy objects that had been carried away from Egypt by the Persians, and he carried them back to Egypt with the rest of the treasure from the region. He sent his forces by way of canals that had been dug....

The text breaks off abruptly after these grandiloquent claims to world conquest, from Thrace on the western shore of the Bosporus all the way to the heartland of the Persian empire as far as modern Afghanistan (Bactriana). It is tempting to believe that Ptolemy wanted this commemorative inscription erected in such a remote spot as Adulis both because this was a region in which he and his father had hunted elephants for military use, and also because he could thereby stake a claim to such a remote territory by frightening off others who might wish to control the area. Certainly the Nubian lands that extended southwards from the Thebaid and the first two cataracts of the Nile could not have been formally subject to the Lagid rulers of Egypt, but they were clearly accessible to them, most probably from the Red Sea but possibly, for seafarers in the Indian Ocean, from the east coast of Africa opposite the Gulf of Aden. Hellenistic settlements on the Red Sea coast at Philotera and Ptolemaïs Thêrôn ("of the Hunts") are both connected with the reign of Ptolemy II Philadelphus, the father of Ptolemy III, and although their foundation cannot be dated with precision, both were clearly designed to facilitate the hunting of elephants.[1]

There remains, of course, the possibility that the Adulis stele was brought to the south at some later time from another place farther to the north, but there can be little doubt that it was already located on the site where Cosmas saw it at the time when the Axumite throne was constructed. This is because the Ptolemaic inscription on the stele so obviously inspired the later text on the throne. Although Adulis is wholly unknown to the historical record for the time of Ptolemy III, it would be perfectly reasonable, in view of its importance for the ivory trade in the Augustan age and later, as reflected both by Juba II and the author of the *Periplus*, to imagine elephant hunting as widespread in the region during the third century BC.[2]

The titulature and filiation of Ptolemy on the inscription, including the names of his incestuous parents (they were brother and sister) as well as the names of their own divinized parents, is exactly as contemporary convention prescribed. Similarly conventional is the use of the adjective *megas*, "great," with Ptolemy's name. This self-aggrandizing adjective deserves special emphasis here because it was not forgotten later by the Ethiopian rulers in the region, who revived it. The cultic designations for brother-sister gods (*theoi adelphoi*) and savior gods (*theoi sôtêres*) are no less accurate than Ptolemy's titulature in reflecting contemporary usage. They properly convey the cultic honors that were given to the royal family at the time. Egyptian rulers appear to have practiced incest without embarrassment and to have celebrated this liaison in deification after death.[3]

The more remote divine ancestry that the inscription provides for Ptolemy—descent from the mythological gods Heracles and Dionysus—may well explain a puzzling item in Cosmas' account of the throne. There he reports that on the back behind the seat, two male images appeared, presumably of divinities and connected in some way with the inscribed text. Cosmas identifies them as Heracles and Hermes, whom his companion interpreted to be symbols of power and wealth, but Cosmas himself speculated most unconvincingly that Hermes ought rather to be understood symbolically as a representation of the divine Word.[4]

The two figures on the back of the throne might at first be thought to represent Heracles and Dionysus because they are the two that were named on the Ptolemaic inscription. But that text had, after all, been inscribed at least three or four centuries before the throne. It still remains possible, however, that the two figures were put there to represent a parallel claim to divine ancestry on the part of the king at Axum, whose inscription is the one that actually appears on the throne. When we turn to that text in the next chapter, it will become apparent that the Axumite ruler must have had the boasts of Ptolemy in mind, because we know that the pre-Christian rulers of Axum had Greek equivalents for their own pagan gods. So the images of two gods on the back of the throne could well owe their origin, in a remote way, to the two who are named in Ptolemy's inscription.

The emphasis on elephants in this text seems to reflect its placement in a part of East Africa where both elephant hunts and trade in ivory were common. That does not of course mean that Ptolemy and his father, or their surrogates, necessarily did their hunting in the immediate vicinity of Adulis. The reference to Troglodytis (more correctly Trogodytis) as well as to Ethiopia indicates that the hunting went on across a very large territory well to the east of the Nile in East Africa.[5] The territory of Trogodytis first appears in the fifth century BC in Herodotus, who called its inhabitants Troglodytes, "cave dwellers," known for running fast, eating snakes, and squealing like bats. He located them vaguely in Ethiopia, but four centuries later the geographer Strabo placed them clearly between the Nile and the Red Sea, and it was in the intervening period between these two writers that Ptolemy III made his allusion to Trogodytis as a region for elephant hunting.[6] The name of Ptolemaïs of the Hunts, which lay on the west coast of the Red Sea, presumably reflects the activity and roughly the chronological period to which Ptolemy refers. In the days of the *Periplus*, a little less than a century after Strabo, the elder Pliny wrote that the Trogodytes, "who live on the border of Ethiopia," made their living exclusively from hunting elephants.[7]

A few documentary texts on papyrus provide tantalizing glimpses into the elephant industry of this period and the compensation paid to those who worked in it. Two are dated to the last years of the reign of Ptolemy III, and one explicitly mentions elephant ships at Berenice, including a ship that had sunk—presumably from its heavy load. An old canal was reopened linking the Nile and the Red Sea to facilitate contacts across the region, and conceivably this was the canal to which Ptolemy alludes in the enigmatic last words that survive from the inscription on the Adulis stele.[8]

The register of overseas territories that Ptolemy inherited from his father, Ptolemy II Philadelphus, is impressive and, to a large extent, supported by textual evidence: Libya (i.e, Cyrenaica), Phoenicia, Syria (so-called Coele or "Hollow" Syria adjacent to Phoenicia), Cyprus, as well as Lycia and Caria in Asia Minor, and the islands of the Cyclades from which Mediterranean piracy could be held in check.[9]

Surprisingly, the inscription returns to elephants in its account of Ptolemaic control of Thrace, where the writer takes care to distinguish the elephants found there as Indian, which were markedly larger animals than the so-called forest elephants that the Ptolemies hunted in Africa. In fact, a decree from Samothrace, honoring a Ptolemaic general, confirms Egyptian control of the Hellespont and Thrace, although it makes no reference to elephants.[10] They presumably arrived there with Alexander's army on its way back from India under Antigonus the One-Eyed during his brief hegemony over Asia Minor and Greece at the end of the fourth century BC.

The occasion for inscribing the stele that Cosmas describes can be determined with considerable precision. Ptolemy's titulature at the beginning lacks the epithet Euergetes ("benefactor"), which we know to have been attached to his name no later than September of 243, whereas the war that took him into Mesopotamia began soon after the death of Antiochus II in 246. Antiochus had been married to Ptolemy's sister Berenice, but not long before he died he divorced his Egyptian queen in favor of the Syrian Laodice. The new queen was established in Ephesus, while the former one remained at Antioch in Syria. Hence, when Antiochus died and was succeeded by Seleucus II, Ptolemy took the opportunity to launch a war to avenge the repudiation of his sister and to weaken Seleucid control in the East wherever possible. Ptolemy arrived in 246 at Seleuceia, the port of Antioch, to great fanfare, according to a famous papyrus document that describes the ceremony, and we know that he then made his way as far as Babylon, where he had to turn back. The invasion of Mesopotamia and the arrival in Babylon are not only attested in ancient literary texts but in a cuneiform document, now in the British Museum, that is a fragment from a Babylonian chronicle.[11] Ptolemy's retreat to Egypt appears to have been, at least in part, caused by sedition at home, but he was certainly back in his kingdom well before he received the title of Euergetes.

Accordingly the events in the Adulis text must be placed between late 246 and 244 BC. There is every sign of gross exaggeration in celebrating Ptolemy's war. The references to Lagid control in Asia Minor do not represent conquests of Ptolemy III himself, but of his predecessors in the third century, and the same can be said of the Ptolemaic presence in the Hellespont and Thrace. Nothing in the ancient tradition, including the new Babylonian chronicle, justifies the claim of reaching Afghanistan.

The Adulis text is thus highly tendentious, possibly one of many efforts to fortify the Egyptian monarchy in the face of the uprising that forced Ptolemy to return to Egypt. By asserting himself in Ethiopia he may have seen a means of securing his southern frontier as well as his control of ports on the Red Sea. The basalt on which the inscription was cut presumably came from the highlands around Axum, which is rich in this volcanic stone, and it argues strongly against any suggestion that the inscription might have been brought to Adulis from somewhere else.

Four centuries, more or less, must have passed between inscribing the basalt stele of Ptolemy III and the dedication of the Axumite marble throne in front of it. Nothing is known of Adulis in those years apart from the ivory trade that is documented in the *Periplus*, which confirms the continuation of elephant hunting in the highlands of Ethiopia. There is no further trace of Ptolemaic presence in the city. The later kings of Hellenistic Egypt would undoubtedly have found it inaccessible at a time when the kingdom of Meroë in upper Nubia, between the fifth and sixth cataracts and corresponding roughly to modern Sudan, became increasingly strong and aggressive as a power to the south of the Ptolemies. Meroë's dominion went back to the seventh century BC, but it grew prosperous from caravan trading in metal, glass, and ivory. Although it had no outlet on the sea, it maintained a grip on products that found their way to the merchants on the coast.

Even Augustus was obliged to turn his attention to Meroë, to which he sent an expedition under C. Petronius, the prefect of Egypt, soon after assuming sole authority at Rome as Princeps, and this happened very soon after he had already sent an unsuccessful expedition under Aelius Gallus, the previous prefect of Egypt, into South Arabia.[12] He realized at that early time in his principate that the economic and political fortunes of both sides of the Red Sea were closely linked. The kings of Axum were soon to discover that the burgeoning Meroitic empire, encompassing the upper Nile as well as the Blue and White Nile, was as much of an obstacle for Ethiopia's access to Egypt as it had been for Augustus in trying to organize Egypt as a Roman province. Like Augustus, the Ethiopian ruler had also eventually to turn his attention to South Arabia. We shall see that the Ethiopian king who celebrated his achievements alongside Ptolemy's almost half a millennium later at Adulis boasted that he had to confront his northern neighbors along the Nile at the very same time as he laid claim to territories in the peninsula on the other side of the Red Sea. This was not only warfare on two fronts, but warfare on two continents. Bringing troops from one to the other involved crossing the Red Sea, and naturally for a king at Axum the best harbor lay in the Gulf of Zula near Adulis.

4

THE KINGDOM OF AXUM

Although Cosmas Indicopleustes failed to recognize that the inscription he found on the Adulis marble throne was part of a totally different document from the one he had transcribed on the Ptolemaic basalt stele, no modern reader of the texts he preserves has had any doubt that the throne text is different and much later. Cosmas unfortunately says nothing about the shapes of the Greek letters on the stone, which might have helped with dating, but it is most unlikely that that the script was similar on the two inscriptions because their historical contexts are very different. Cosmas and his collaborator probably had to struggle so hard with deciphering the letters on these old blocks that it never occurred to them that they were transcribing two separate documents. The text on the throne points unmistakably to a great Ethiopian ruler, even if the ruler's name is missing (as, fortunately, it is not on the stele inscription). The Ethiopian's conquests had taken him not only to the territories north of his kingdom but also to the land of Ḥimyar in southwest Arabia on the other side of the Red Sea. Since we know from extant inscriptions that the principal deity of the pagan Ethiopian kings, Maḥrem, was always equated with the Greek Ares,[1] the dedication of the Adulis throne to the god Ares, together with the traditional form of an inscribed votive throne, proves definitively that the anonymous dedicant was none other than the *negus* in Axum. The identification of Maḥrem with Ares presumably implies that he was some kind of war-god, as Ares was, and that he was invoked in gratitude for Ethiopian conquest. But this can be no more than speculation.

About the general epoch of the throne and its dedication there can be no doubt. It must certainly be later than that of the king called Zoskales in the *Periplus of the Red Sea*. The territory of Zoskales, whatever its precise contours, did not extend to the Arabian peninsula, and it is far from certain that his royal seat was in Axum.[2] But it is clear from the *Periplus* that he knew and used the Greek language with proficiency, and this was the indispensable prerequisite for the composition of the long inscription on the throne, as recorded by Cosmas. Even when the rulers in Axum later set up inscriptions in Ethiopic (Ge'ez), they continued to use Greek as a kind of lingua franca. They did this on their coinage as well.[3] Although much remains unclear, particularly in the interpretation of toponyms, it is certain that the text Cosmas saw is undoubtedly the earliest of all known Axumite royal inscriptions.

Unfortunately its opening lines are lost. It is altogether unlike the Ptolemaic document, but, in conformity with all the inscriptions we know to have been set up by the kings of Axum, it is written in the first person. The first surviving words, which, in the original, must have followed a prescript with the identity and titles of the king who is speaking, allude back to unnamed events, after which the speaker "grew to manhood," or perhaps "gained in strength." The precise meaning of the participle *andreiôsas*, implying manhood or manly strength, cannot be determined. The inscription reads as follows:

> . . . afterwards I grew to manhood and bade the nations closest to my kingdom to keep peace. I waged war and subjugated in battle the following peoples.
>
> I fought the tribe of Gaze, then won victories over the Agame and Siguene. I took as my share half their property and their population. The Aua, Zingabene, Aggabe, Tiamaa, Athagaoi, Kalaa, and Samene, people who live beyond the Nile in inaccessible and snowy mountains, in which there are storms, and ice and snow so deep that a man sinks in up to his knees—these people I subjugated after crossing the river. Then I subjugated the inhabitants of Lasine, Zaa, and Gabala who live by a mountain with bubbling and flowing streams of hot waters. I subjugated the Atalmo and Beja and all the peoples of the Tangaitai with them, who dwell as far as the frontiers of Egypt. I made passable the road from the places of my kingdom all the way to Egypt. Then I

subdued the inhabitants of Annene and Metine on craggy mountains.

I fought the Sesea people, who had gone up onto the greatest and most inaccessible mountain. I surrounded them and brought them down, and I chose for myself their young men, women, boys, girls, and all their property. I subjugated the peoples of Rauso who live in the midst of incense-gathering Barbarians between great waterless plains, and I subjugated the people of Solate, whom I ordered to guard the coasts of the sea. All these people, enclosed by mighty mountains, I myself conquered in person in battle and brought them under my rule. I allowed them the use of all their lands in return for the payment of tribute. Many other peoples voluntarily subjected themselves to me by paying tribute.

I sent both a fleet and an army of infantry against the Arabitai and the Kinaidocolpitai who dwell across the Red Sea, and I brought their kings under my rule. I commanded them to pay tax on their land and to travel in peace by land and sea. I made war from Leukê Kômê to the lands of the Sabaeans.

I was the first and only king of any down to my time to subjugate all these peoples. That is why I express my gratitude to my greatest god, Ares, who also begat me, through whom I brought under my sway all the peoples who are adjacent to my land, on the east as far as the Land of Incense and on the west as far as the

> places of Ethiopia and Sasou. Some I went and conquered in person, others by dispatching expeditions. Having imposed peace on the entire world under me, I went down to Adulis to sacrifice to Zeus, to Ares, and to Poseidon on behalf of those who go under sail. Once I had brought together my forces and united them, I encamped in this place and made this throne as a dedication to Ares in the 27th year of my reign.

This extraordinary document marks the beginning of our knowledge of the kingdom of Axum and provides a detailed account of the foreign policy of the anonymous king. The identification of many of the names for places and peoples remains uncertain and open to inconclusive debate,[4] but some of the names can be linked with known toponyms and peoples so that a relatively clear picture of the king's realm after his conquests can be worked out. The wars all concern territories adjacent to Ethiopia. The sequence implies a geographical movement extending beyond the borders of the kingdom in all directions, and an overseas expedition across the Red Sea brought the troops of this ruler into conflict with the peoples on the western side of the Arabian peninsula. This obvious attempt to secure not only the borders of the African kingdom on all sides, but the coastal areas lying opposite on the Red Sea, suggests a concerted effort to establish Ethiopian control over East Africa and the trade that passed through its ports. The king's boast that he opened up a land route all the way to Egypt reinforces the impression that his objectives were as much commercial as defensive.

The register of conquests in the surviving part of the inscription begins with the territories that lay northeast of Axum. These include "the tribe of Gaze," which can be located in the region called Agazi (Aga'aze) in the plateau overlooking the sea north of Massawa. The king began his many wars with the tribe that was closest to home, just north of Axum itself, and he presumably launched his campaign directly from the capital. By his own report he then moved on against the Agame and Siguene, half of whose property and population he took over for his own. Agame was equally close by, to the north of Axum, and its name may possibly survive in the modern toponym of Adigrat. The location of Siguene remains a mystery, although there can be no doubt that it too was not far from Axum to the north. Littmann's proposed identification with the modern Soguet, near Adigrat, is at least plausible.

From the Eritrean plain the king appears to have extended his belligerent activities to the south into Tigray, and the site of Aua may indicate the modern capital of the region, Adwa. The Byzantine diplomat Nonnosus explicitly mentions Aua as lying on the way from Adulis to Axum. He was a traveler of infinite curiosity and took pains to record the remarkable scenes that confronted him as he made his way to Axum from the port at Adulis. The open territory at Aua greatly impressed Nonnosus and his companions because it contained a large number of elephants, "almost five thousand," which were grazing in a vast space that the local inhabitants could enter only with difficulty.[5] The names of the next conquests of the Axumite king, Zingabene and Aggabe, remain obscure to this day, and scholarly speculation has been impeded by an error in an ancient gloss that Tiamaa, which is the next name in the list, indicated the Takkaze towards the Nile to the northwest. This cannot be right, but the mistake has led to placing the no less obscure Athagaous in the same area. The king is evidently still referring to the tribal regions he invaded as he moved southwards into the Ethiopian highlands, as Littmann was again alert to notice.

If Kalaa resists identification, however, Samene, which follows it in the list, does not. This is incontestably the mountainous territory of Simēn, which lies southwest of Axum to the east of the Atbara river above the fifth cataract of the Nile and rises to snowy heights that perfectly fit the king's description of storms and deep snowdrifts. It is undoubtedly this river that he crossed before subduing the region, and when he refers to its inhabitants as living beyond the Nile he can only mean the Atbara offshoot of the Nile. In these opening campaigns the king thus secured control of the peoples that inhabited the borderlands both to the north and south of his capital city. This embraced a large swath of land from the Red Sea coast in the vicinity of Asmara and Massawa to the mountains of Simēn—a considerable achievement.

Next the king targeted regions farther north, as far as Egypt itself. Although the territories along the way, Lasine, Zaa, and Gabala, are unknown, the reference to hot springs point to precisely such waters that can be found north of Axum at Mansa and Habab. Although the next stop at Atalmo is also unknown, Beja brings us into recognizable territory. The people there were well known in classical sources under the name of Blemmyes, occupying a broad area of the interior near the coast of East Africa and south of the Hellenistic port city of Berenice. The Tangaites, who appear next in the king's register, were a powerful tribe of the Beja and confirm that the king's wars now brought him into the land of East Africa southwest of Berenice. There is not the slightest reason to see him as campaigning farther west into the kingdom of Meroë, although it is more than likely that the strength of this powerful kingdom was, as we will see, a matter of concern to him. The sequence of wars described thus far readily prepares the reader of his inscription for the revelation that the Axumite king next established a land route between Axum and Egypt. It is this development, more than any other, that proves Axum was not merely interested in protecting its borders but also in the commerce that flowed through East Africa to the Red Sea.

After the conquests that brought the king within range of the Egyptian frontier, he turned his attention to five other regions, Annene, Metine, Sesea, Rauso, and Solate. All are unknown, and guesses about the toponyms have hitherto been unproductive. Nevertheless, the descriptions of the intervening terrain allow, within the geographical framework of the king's narrative, for reasonable speculation. Sesea includes an inaccessible mountain, Rauso evokes people "who live in the midst of incense-gathering Barbarians between great waterless plains," and Solate is obviously close to the seacoast, which it is ordered to protect. That very high mountain can only lie southeast of the mountainous Simēn, where the king had already fought, and the allusion to waterless plains suggests that he moved yet farther to the southeast into Djibouti or Somalia. The incense-gathering barbarians must therefore be residents of the land called Barbaria, rather than simply savages, inasmuch as this region lay roughly in the area of Somalia. The city of Berbera on the Somali coast preserves the ancient name.

In view of their harvesting incense, the barbarians of the inscription take us clearly to the Land of Incense that is mentioned near the end of the inscribed text under that name. This is certainly a reference to Barbaria, covering roughly Djibouti and Somalia. The area stretched out south of the Axumite kingdom precisely where the *Periplus* had located the domain of Zoskales. The king finally completed his tour of conquest by approaching the coast, perhaps on the Gulf of Aden at or below the Bab al Mandeb. There he established guard-stations wherever Solate may have been.

His wars, as they are represented in his inscription, can be seen to have been systematically organized, beginning with the northern territories above Axum and extending towards Egypt on the north and the Red Sea on the east. After taking control there and securing a route into Egypt itself, the king swung southwestwards into the mountains below Axum, and from there moved further south and east into still higher mountains, to emerge at last into the incense-bearing plains of Barbaria and the coast.

The king nowhere mentions the rival Nubian kingdom of Meroë under that name, but it was obviously much on his mind. His boast that he had opened up an accessible route to the Egyptian border from his own kingdom can only mean that he had found a way to reach Egypt by going around the Nubians on their eastern flank. Furthermore, when he concludes by saying that the western extremities of his realm reached Ethiopia, he obviously cannot be referring to his own kingdom under that name but must rather be referring to the Meroitic kingdom in Nubia, which, since the time of Herodotus, had traditionally been known as Ethiopia.[6] No less traditional is the use of the name Barbaroi for the inhabitants of modern Somalia. As we have already seen, these are not barbarians in the Greek sense of non-Greeks but rather the eponymous people of the territory of Barbaria as we know it from the *Periplus*. Although the etymology of the name Barbaroi has nothing to do with the Greek *barbaros*, it is undoubtedly related to the ethnic name Berber, which, as we know from the great fourteenth-century Arab historian Ibn Khaldun, arose in a way not unlike Greek *barbaros*.[7] The language these people spoke sounded to a foreigner like *bar-bar* or *ber-ber*. The author of the *Periplus of the Red Sea* guarantees that the East-African Barbaroi were to be found in the region of Somalia, where King Zoskales was, according to the merchant manual, the ruler of lands "from the Moscophagoi ["calf-eaters" in the north] to the rest of Barbaria."[8] The existence of a temple of Barbar on the island of Bahrain in the Persian Gulf raises the possibility that a divinity may have been associated with the name in Somalia.

So the nomenclature of the throne inscription reflects the world that was already known to the author of the *Periplus* in the mid-first century of our era. It also maintains the very old Herodotean tradition of referring to Nubia as Ethiopia, a name that alludes to its dark-skinned people who had "burnt faces" (*aithiopes*). This etymology for Ethiopia continued to be in vogue throughout the second and early third centuries, as can be seen by references to the Ethiopians as blacks in Philostratus' *Life of Apollonius of Tyana*—a work that also perpetuates the view that Nubia with its capital Meroë constituted Ethiopia.[9] Gradually the kingdom of Axum assumed the separate name of Ethiopia as the kingdom of Meroë became conventionally identified by that name in Greek and by Kush in Semitic languages. Kush, however, also continued to designate the kingdom of Ethiopia, particularly in Syriac apocalyptic literature, exactly as the Greek name had done formerly.[10]

The Adulis inscription looks very much as if it comes from the time of transition in the use of the name of Ethiopia. Philostratus was writing in the early third century AD about events in the late first century AD, and so this gives an approximate range of the second to the third century. Accordingly, a much neglected passage in an often cited work, the panegyric *To Rome* by the Greek sophist Aelius Aristides, becomes surprisingly relevant. In praising Rome's administration of its empire, the orator says that wars have now passed and peace reigns, but this stands in contrast to recent troubles that he mentions explicitly: "the immoderate paranoia of the Getae, the misery of the Libyans, and the wickedness of peoples who live along the Red Sea."[11] Aristides' speech belongs probably to 144, or possibly somewhat later, but the forties of the second century are clearly evoked by this modest list of international incidents. The episode with the Getae, who lived in Dacia (modern Romania), points to events precisely in 144, as does the misery in Libya (here used vaguely for North Africa), which must allude to disturbances in Mauretania at about the same time.[12] The reference to the Red Sea, which has long been obscure to anyone who bothered to notice it, is now illuminated by a Latin inscription found in the Farasan archipelago in the Red Sea off the coast of Arabia. This reveals the presence of Roman legionary detachments—a *vexillatio* and *auxilia*—responding to some kind of crisis in the region. The titulature of the emperor Antoninus Pius establishes a date between late December of 143 and late December of 144.[13] Of course there is no way of telling what the problem was, and the panegyrist would have us believe that it had been resolved. But we are not obliged to see this as anything more than an indication that the problem had been addressed, and if the Roman force was actually stationed in islands in the Red Sea it may be suspected that the disruptions involved naval activity of some kind.

Hence a date for the Adulis throne in or a little before the third century, on the basis of the language it deploys, can be strengthened by the new Farasan inscription. But more than that: it is supported by the startling references of the anonymous king himself to the overseas campaigns that he waged in South Arabia, in the area of modern Yemen and the coastal Tihāma of Saudi Arabia. After the sweep of his conquests to the north and south of Axum, the king turned to the other side of the Red Sea. It is in Sabaic epigraphy of the early third century that the earliest attestations of the presence of Axumite forces in this region occur.[14] At that time the occupying Axumites are designated by the Sabaic word for Ethiopians, *ḥabashat,* and its king bears the name Gadara. This king appears in the Sabaic epigraphy of South Arabia between

200 and 230 AD, and, most remarkably, he also appears on an inscription in Ethiopia itself as the *negus* of Aksum. He is the first attested ruler with that title. By contrast the Arabian inscriptions call him king, with the Sabaic *malik*.[15] Surviving documentary evidence for the Ethiopian presence in South Arabia has suggested to recent scholars that the Ethiopians remained in the peninsula until about 270. But the expedition that installed the Ethiopians there—the expedition described in the Adulis inscription—must belong to the very first decades of the third century, or perhaps even a little earlier.[16]

This chronology fits perfectly with the appearance of the Kinaidocolpitai in the inscription. These enigmatic people bear a name that is inexplicably obscene if understood as Greek (*kinaidos* is a pathic homosexual). The element *colpitai* in their name points to their dwelling on or near a gulf or bay (*kolpos*). They appear rarely in ancient texts, but the few attestations that exist point clearly to the second and third centuries. Apart from the Adulis inscription and a Byzantine lexicon they are found only in Ptolemy's *Geography* from the mid-second century AD, on an ostracon from Arabia that is also from the mid-second century, and in a chronicle of Saint Hippolytus from 234.[17] The location of these people was clearly in the center of the western part of the Arabian peninsula, which is exactly where we should expect to find them on the basis of the Adulis text. The northernmost city in that text is Leukê Kômê, perhaps modern Wajh but in any case north of the apparent territory of the Kinaidocolpitai. These people disappear altogether from the historical record after the mid-third century. They reappear only in the Byzantine age in an entry of a comprehensive lexicon of ethnic names, where they are identified as a people in Arabia Felix, which is hardly surprising because Arabia Felix is the Arabian peninsula.[18] So the presence of the Kinaidocolpitai, mysterious as their name may be, serves effectively to confirm a late second or early third century date for the Adulis throne inscription.

What remains uncertain after anchoring the date of the Adulis inscription to this period is the identity of the *negus* himself. He boasts that he was the "first and only" king to have done what he did, and we have to ask whether Gadara, who is known both from Arabia and from Ethiopia at this time, is that person. On present evidence there is just one other candidate for Adulis' anonymous king. That is a certain Sembrouthes, whom we know from a carefully incised Greek inscription found north of Asmara in Eritrea.[19] He styles himself "king from Axumite kings" (*basileus ek basileôn Axômeitôn*) and so he obviously had predecessors, just as the author of the Adulis text who boasted that he was the "first and only" king to make such conquests. But Sembrouthes also calls himself "great" (*megas*), as Ptolemy III had done on the basalt stele near the throne. Since we lack the prescript for the throne inscription, it is impossible to know whether the anonymous king of that text called himself *megas* too, but it is probable that he did. Furthermore, Sembrouthes declares that he was in the twenty-fourth year of his reign when he set up his inscription, and on present evidence long reigns at Axum were uncommon. Yet the Adulis king had an even longer reign since he claims to have written in his twenty-seventh year. The Greek letter-forms on Sembrouthes' inscription are large and clear, and they could belong anywhere in the second or third centuries AD. They are therefore wholly consistent with the period of Ethiopian occupation in South Arabia.

Identifying the anonymous king at Adulis as Gadara would be credible because he is the only Ethiopian ruler who is actually documented both in Arabia itself and in Ethiopia at this time. Such an identification would fit well with the conquests enumerated on the inscription.[20] On the other hand, Sembrouthes' title *megas* is echoed in the Ptolemaic titulature at Adulis, and that titulature, like so much else on that old stele, presumably inspired the throne's anonymous king. In his brief prescript Sembrouthes describes himself with the exalted language "king of Axumite kings." But he conspicuously does not use the more traditional formulation "king of kings" that was later used by the Axumite kings and is most often associated with Persia. Sembrouthes' Greek *basileus ek basileôn* ("king from kings"), rather than the customary *basileus basileôn* ("king of kings") may conceivably point to a royal lineage for Sembrouthes, rather than a claim to be a king who ranks above other kings.

What is particularly remarkable about the conquests of the king who dedicated the Adulis throne is that he now appears, with a fair degree of certainty, to have put up three other Greek inscriptions—one in Axum itself, and, more remarkably, two in Nubian Meroë. These texts, fragmentary as they are, also lack the royal name, but their allusions to expeditions across the sea point unmistakably to the Adulis king. The inscription at Axum explicitly refers to crossing the sea, and it also mentions infantry transported in the expedition.[21] The text boasts that the enterprise is the "first," and it records a dedication to Ares. The two Greek inscriptions at Meroë look very much as if they were put up by the same ruler with reference to the same expedition.[22] One Meroitic stone mentions both Axumites and Ḥimyarites (the people of Ḥimyar in southwestern Arabia), and it also mentions generals and the payment of tribute. The other, which is extremely fragmentary, contains just enough to show another dedication of a throne to Ares. It is more than likely that these texts have combined allusions to the king's Arabian campaign with the imposition of tribute in the territory of Meroë. Whether the *negus* behind all this was Gadara or Sembrouthes, he is manifestly the Adulis king. The name of this energetic ruler is ultimately less important than the secure assignment of the events on the Adulis inscription to a dated historical context. These events marked the beginning of some seventy years of Ethiopian occupation in the Arabian peninsula in the third century AD.

The significance of two inscriptions set up in Greek by an Ethiopian *negus* in Meroë is immense. The Meroitic kingdom was undoubtedly in decline at this period, and the last known attestation of a Meroitic king is a graffito on the Nile island of Philae from 260. Although a few later graffiti show that some Nubians from this kingdom were still traveling, the great days of prosperity from the caravans that transported goods across Egypt between the Mediterranean and the Red Sea seem to have ended by 320 or so.[23] An ambitious *negus* would have sensed a golden opportunity in the realm to his northwest. Since the *negus* of the Adulis inscription had clearly not yet invaded Meroë at the time it was incised on the throne, the fragmentary texts that survived in the Nubian capital must indicate further expansion to the northwest of the territories that Axum already controlled. The allusions to the overseas war and the phrasing that accompanies them both echo and postdate the Adulis text.

The message conveyed by the two Greek inscriptions at Meroë is reinforced by the imagination of the brilliant novelist Heliodorus, whose fictional narrative, the *Aethiopica*, shows revealing anachronisms in the midst of a story that was purportedly set in the sixth or fifth century BC. At a great celebration in Meroë the king Hydaspes receives gifts from foreign delegations.[24] Those that are named have nothing whatever to do with the fictional date of Heliodorus' tale but everything to do with the world in which he was writing, probably the fourth century AD or just possibly the third. The ambassadors to Meroë represent the regional powers of that time. They come from the Arabian peninsula (*Arabia Felix*), from the Blemmyes (the Beja of the Adulis inscription), who dwelled alongside the Meroitic kingdom, and most strikingly the Axumites.[25] The presence of Chinese (Seres) bearing silk could conceivably reflect knowledge of the silk trade in the Roman Empire, but there can be no doubt at all that the Arabians and Axumites provide a glimpse into the world of the very king who described his conquests in the text on the Adulis throne as well as into his further conquests after he wrote it.

As already noted, the departure of the Ethiopians can be assigned to about 270 on the basis of the Arabian inscriptions, which reveal the restoration of authority to local tribes in Arabia. Interestingly, it is precisely at the time of the Ethiopian withdrawal back to East Africa that the kings of Axum chose to consolidate their rule at home by inaugurating a coinage in gold, silver, and bronze with the names and busts of the kings themselves. Names on the coins were generally rendered in Greek, although one king, Wazeba, who is otherwise unknown, added unvocalized Ethiopic to the Greek legends.[26] No inscriptions on stone survive from the kings who first issued coins, but the consistency of their images, with a close-fitting headcloth, suggest a deliberate effort *not* to represent the king as a Greek despite the use of the Greek language. By the early fourth century the imperial head had acquired a magnificent crown, as can be seen on the obverse of a series of gold coins issued by the *basileus* Ousanas, but the reverse of these issues continued to show the king with a traditional headcloth.[27] The crown is absent from his silver and bronze coins. It was Ousanas' successor Aezanas ('Ezānā) who was the first in the fourth century to set up numerous inscriptions, and from him we discover the grandiose irredentist claim of the Ethiopians to the Arabian territory that Ethiopia had formerly occupied.

It is clear that the memory of Ḥimyar had never died despite the Ethiopian withdrawal from the Arabian peninsula in the third century. Aezanas never carried out any overseas conquests, but he did not hesitate to declare himself proudly "King of the Aksumites and Ḥimyarites, of Raydān, Ethiopians, Sabaeans, Silene, Siyamo, Beja (Blemmyes), and Kush (Meroë), King of Kings, son of the invincible god Ares (Maḥrem)."[28] This is truly a "king of kings" and not, like Sembrouthes, a "king from kings." The claim to Ḥimyar and Raydān was pure fiction, as these territories lay in southwestern Arabia, where the *negus* had no control whatever at that time. But the other regions lay to the north and west of Axum in East Africa and may well have represented, to some degree, his power in the region. Certainly by this time Meroë had become increasingly weak as rival Nubian peoples were growing stronger to the north, and Axum had already moved in to assert its authority there. On the whole Aezanas' titles seem to have represented an ambitious program for the future.

5

CHRISTIANITY COMES TO AXUM

Exactly what drove the Ethiopians out of Arabia around 270 is just as obscure as what brought them there in the first place. Imperialist expansionism, probably nourished by a desire to control both sides of the Red Sea and the commercial traffic that sailed along it, would be a reasonable explanation of their arrival. But in any case by the end of the third century the Ethiopians were out of the territories of Saba and Ḥimyar in the southwest of the peninsula, which returned to the rule of their indigenous peoples. The names for the various regions varied, presumably as the centers of power reflected the places and cults of diverse Arab tribes. One region, in the Ḥaḍramawt, became known as Dhū Raydān, to indicate that it belonged to a pagan divinity called Raydān. This was not long before what is known today as the Kingdom of Ḥimyar with its capital at

Zaphār emerged out of these various territories.[1] It was this kingdom that the Ethiopians had occupied, and it was this kingdom that dominated the memory of the rulers in Axum after the Ethiopian withdrawal from Arabia.

As the Ethiopian kings consolidated their power in their East African homeland, they not only instituted mints for a coinage in all three metals, as we have seen, but arrogated titles that asserted sovereignty in the Arabian peninsula even though they no longer ruled there. They never forgot where they had been. In a spirit of both nostalgia and irredentism, the *negus* represented himself as "king of kings," ruler over Axum and Ḥimyar, as well as over Dhū Raydān in the Ḥaḍramawt, and Saba in Yemen. He also made claims to sovereignty within East Africa at the borders of his own kingdom, and although these may have had more validity they cannot be verified. In the fourth century he had no hesitation in registering among his subjects many of the peoples that the anonymous king on the Adulis inscription proclaimed that he had conquered, including those he actually called Ethiopians (probably an allusion to the waning Meroitic kingdom), as well as Blemmyes and other peoples adjacent to Axum.

These royal assertions of sovereignty in the fourth century, echoing those at Adulis and including the phrase "king of kings," appear considerably after Sembrouthes' boast, from a century or more earlier, of being a "king from kings." Although the expression "king of kings" is well known from the Persian monarchy, there is not the slightest reason to think that its appearance in Ethiopia was due to any direct influence from Persia, but the phrase had a certain currency in the eastern Roman

Empire. The Pontic kingdoms of the time also had rulers who called themselves "king of kings."[2] This was when they were operating wholly outside the Persian orbit, and, in fact, most of the attestations of this title in the Pontic realms occur before the Sassanian Persians expelled the Parthian monarchy from its Iranian homeland in 224 AD. At Palmyra in the later third century "king of kings" even turns up for two local rulers at this powerful mercantile center in the Syrian desert. It cannot be excluded that the rulers in Axum were inspired indirectly by an awareness of the Sassanian fondness for the title *shah-in-shah*, or king of kings, but it seems far more likely that this expression arose locally in Ethiopia as a development from the phrase that Sembrouthes used when he declared himself to be a king *from* kings.

The extensive epigraphy of Aezanas, or ʿEzana, reveals the full titulature of the *negus* in the fourth century. His inscriptions allow us to follow his career from the time when he was a great pagan ruler, claiming to be the son of the god Ares, who was equated with the Ethiopian Maḥrem, down to his later years as a devout Christian ruler who announced that he owed his kingship to God.[3] The evolving titulature of Aezanas reflects the coming of Christianity to Axum.

The appearance of Christianity at the court did nothing to alter the irredentist claims of the *negus*, even as he transferred his allegiance from the traditional Ares (Maḥrem) to the newly adopted Christian God. The inscriptions of Aezanas imply clearly that his various texts all drew their inspiration from earlier royal documents of which the one on the Adulis throne is our sole surviving example. Aezanas is the most prominent of all the Axumite kings who reigned between the Adulis inscription and the sixth-century *negus* for whom Cosmas copied the inscriptions at Adulis when he was visiting the town. We shall see that Cosmas' sixth-century king saw an opportunity to turn Aezanas' hollow claims to Arabian territory into geopolitical reality. The first step in making this possible had been the conversion of Aezanas himself to Christianity.

Ecclesiastical legend, as preserved in the church historian Rufinus, attributed the Christianization of Axum to a certain Frumentius from Alexandria.[4] A romantic story of his capture as a boy by Ethiopian pirates off the coast of East Africa, at a place presumed to be near Adulis, need not be believed, but the presence in Axum of someone by the name of Frumentius is securely documented in the *Apology* that Athanasius addressed to the Byzantine emperor Constantius II in 356. This was sent after one of Athanasius' numerous expulsions from his seat as orthodox archbishop at Alexandria in direct consequence of hostility from the Arians. It is obvious from Athanasius' carefully crafted *Apology* that Frumentius had been in Axum for a considerable period and was by that time bishop of a Christian community there that now included the king himself. The *Apology* quotes verbatim a letter that Constantius had sent to both Aezanas and his brother demanding that Frumentius, whom Athanasius had instructed for his bishopric, be returned to Alexandria for fresh instruction at the hands of the new Arian patriarch George.[5] Apart from demonstrating Constantius' hostility to Athanasius and to the orthodox creed he espoused, the emperor's letter to Axum, as quoted in the

Apology, leaves no doubt that he and perhaps Constantine before him had approved, or at least accepted, the Christianizing mission of Frumentius to the Ethiopians.

The date of the conversion of Aezanas is irrecoverable, but the suggestion of Stuart Munro-Hay that it had already happened by 340 is not unreasonable.[6] It had certainly happened when Constantius II acquired sole power over the Mediterranean empire from 343 onwards, and it was only the exile of Athanasius in 356 that precipitated the demand for Frumentius' return to Alexandria for new instruction in Arian theology. These doctrinal issues cannot be discerned in the language of Aezanas' inscriptions that span the great divide from paganism to Christianity. But the conceptualization of the Axumite kingship as the gift of Ares (Maḫrem) and subsequently the Christian God is unambiguous.

It is by no means clear why Aezanas, even as a pagan ruler, appears to have been so much more loquacious on stone than most of his forebears. But the aggressive tone of his documents unmistakably reveals an ambitious ruler with an ambitious agenda. The inscribed stones he left behind are large rectangular blocks. The excavators who worked at Axum during the German archaeological expedition to the site in the early years of the twentieth century believed that many of these large, inscribed slabs were, as appears likely for some stones conveying Aezanas' achievements in different scripts, the sidepieces on commemorative thrones. Some thirty bases for thrones of this kind survive.[7] In other words, they would be closely parallel in design to the inscribed stones that comprised the throne that Cosmas saw at Adulis. It is even possible that many of Aezanas' inscriptions served this purpose, and the evident duplication of one of the most remarkable inscriptions from his pagan years would best be explained by the existence of two separate thrones for them.

This pagan inscription is found on two unconnected stones at Axum with the same inscribed texts cut on both faces. The first and best known of these two stones was seen and copied in part by H. Salt in 1805. Subsequently, Theodore Bent saw it and made squeezes, and in 1906 the Germans copied and photographed all the texts on this stone, and also made impressions on paper ("squeezes") for future reference.[8] The writing on one face is Greek, but on the other Ge'ez, written twice but in different scripts. The upper text is in Sabaic *musnad* script, going from right to left, and the lower text is in unvocalized Ethiopic, going from left to right. There are thus three versions of the text on a single slab, one in Greek and two in Ge'ez (though in different scripts). Amazingly, in 1981 another stone turned up at Axum with the very same texts inscribed in the same two languages, and again with two different scripts for the Ge'ez (*Fig. 3*).[9] The newly discovered stone clarified points that had previously been unclear on the earlier stone because of substantial erosion.

All three texts are presented as the words of Aezanas himself, called "king of the Axumites, Homerites (Ḥimyarites), Raydān, Ethiopians, Sabaeans, Silene, Siyamo, Beja (Blemmyes), and Kasou." After next declaring himself a "king of kings" and, in the Greek a son of Ares, or in the Ge'ez a son of Maḥrem, he says that he sent his brothers Saiazanas and Adiphas to make war against the Blemmyes to the north of his

Figure 3. Inscription at Axum, commemorating the achievements of Aezanas in classical Ethiopic (Ge'ez), written in South Arabian Sabaic script. The text appears in *RIE* Vol. 1, no. 185 bis, text II, face B, p. 247. Photo courtesy of Finbarr Barry Flood.

kingdom. Aezanas furnishes a detailed account of the terms of submission of these peoples and expresses his gratitude by means of offerings "to him who brought me forth, the invincible Ares (or Maḥrem)." A royal text in Greek is hardly surprising in view of the consistent use of Greek on the Ethiopian coinage, nor is it surprising to find a text in Ethiopic letters inasmuch as this was the local script for the Ge'ez language. But it is far less obvious what Aezanas had in mind when he had the same text inscribed in Ge'ez in the Sabaic *musnad* of South Arabia. It is true that the Ethiopic letters were derived from Sabaic letters, but they were by now substantially different and were normally written from left to right, as Sabaic writing was not. The Ge'ez in Sabaic script does include a few minor variations from the vocabulary in Ethiopic, most conspicuously in the first two lines where the word king appears in Sabaic as *mlk*, but in Ethiopic as *ngś*. Furthermore, the Sabaic text of the Ge'ez preserves the Sabaic *mimation* (the addition of the letter mim at the end of nouns), which is conspicuously absent in Ethiopic.

We can watch the process of Aezanas' ultimate conversion to Christianity played out in the texts of two other public inscriptions, one in Ge'ez that has been known since 1840, and another in Greek, first published in 1970 but closely related in time and substance to the Ge'ez text. The Ethiopic script (*fidal*) of the Ge'ez inscription appears with full vocalization and begins with the highly innovative prefix, "In the power of the Lord of Heaven, who is victorious in heaven and on earth for me, I Aezanas . . ."[10] The speaker's name, filiation, and titles follow, including claims to the kingship of both Axum and Ḥimyar in Arabia and Salhēn and Beja (the Blemmyes) in East Africa. He goes on a few lines later to declare, "In the power of the Lord of all, I went to war against the Noba when the peoples had rebelled and boasted of it . . ., In the power of the Lord I made war by the river Atbara at the ford Kemalke, and they fled." The Ge'ez word for river here (*takazi*) functioned as a proper name for the Atbara that linked with the Nile above the fifth cataract. Some thirty lines on Aezanas declares, "I set up a throne at the confluence of the rivers Nile and Atbara" as a tangible commemoration of the victories he describes. Towards the end of the same inscription Aezanas again invokes the Lord of Heaven in gratitude for having given the king his rule by destroying his enemies, and he beseeches Him to strengthen it. By setting up the throne at Axum, as well as on the Nile where it joined the Atbara, the *negus* is following a custom that had, as the Adulis throne exemplifies, deep roots in the pagan past. Aezanas attributes his successes to the Lord of Heaven (or sometimes simply Lord), but no longer to any pagan deity.

At the end of the inscription Aezanas declares that his Lord is the one "who made me king and the earth that bears it [the throne]." This last phrase has been thought to be a faint echo of pre-Christian consecrations of a votive throne to Maḥrem. But in fact the various formulations of the divine power—Lord of Heaven, Lord of all, and simply Lord—refer unmistakably to the Christian God. The single word, meaning literally Lord of the Land (Egziabeḥēr), is in fact the standard name for God in the Ethiopic Bible and should be rendered as such. But the most striking feature of Aezanas' inscription is that it nowhere mentions Jesus Christ or the Trinity.

His allusions in this text to his war with the Noba show how much the geopolitical situation had changed in the Sudanese area since the end of the previous century. It was in 298 that the emperor Diocletian had gone to Egypt and addressed the problems his government faced from the tribes in upper Egypt and, to the south of it, in lower Nubia. The imperial frontier in the region had been at Hiera Sykaminos south of Syene (Aswan), and it enclosed the territory known as Dodekaschoinos ("Twelve Mile Land") along the Nile. But the emperor observed that the expense of policing the area with Roman troops was not balanced by the revenues that were coming into the treasury, and so he astutely decided to solve the problem by pulling the frontier back to Syene (Aswan) and putting the African tribe of Nobatai into the Dodekaschoinos district. This tribe had been causing havoc by plundering the oasis area of the Thebaid, and so Diocletian found he could eliminate both this vexation and the unprofitability of the southern frontier by transplanting the Nobatai into good land along the Nile that they were glad to have.[11] This migration of the Nobatai served also, as Diocletian had expected, to curtail the depredations of the Blemmyes, who had been another troublesome tribe for the new emperor. They were forced southeast into territory where they could be held in check by the Nobatai who were now on both sides of the Nile (*Map 1*).

To solidify the resettlement agreement the emperor decreed that a fixed amount of gold should be paid annually to the Nobatai and the Blemmyes alike to keep them from plundering the adjacent Roman territory to the north of the new frontier at Syene. This was an exceptionally clever reorganization on Diocletian's part, and it meant that lower Nubia now lay outside the Roman Empire. Because the kingdom at Meroë had already collapsed by this time, the land to the north and west of the capital, particularly in the great arc of the Nile between the fourth and fifth cataracts, was now available for the tribe of the Noba to move into. These were the people against whom the Christian Aezanas found it necessary to make war in the middle of the fourth century. They were obviously attempting to fill the power vacuum left by the fall of Meroë.

In contrast with the absence of references to Christ or the Trinity in the Ethiopic text that dates from the time of

Aezanas' conversion, the inscription that he set up in Greek displays overtly Christian protocols as well as a partial record of the same conquests. It is much less oblique. This is either because it came a little later or, more probably, because Aezanas felt he could be more open in the official language of eastern Christianity than in his own native Ge'ez. The two texts are manifestly related, as scholars have recognized ever since the publication of the Greek, and they cannot be very far apart in time even though they differ in the manner in which Aezanas chose to make his conversion public. The Greek text begins, "In trust in God and in the power of the Father, Son, and Holy Ghost, for His salvation of my kingdom through faith in His Son, Jesus Christ." The *negus* calls himself a *doulos Christi* (slave/servant of Christ), and continues to speak of his indebtedness to God and to Christ. He says that because of the complaints of various tribes "I went forth to fight against the Noba, and I rose up in the power of God–Christ (*tou theou Christou*), in Whom I trusted, and He guided me." The account of the Noba is much more succinct here than in the Ethiopic inscription, but the acknowledgment of divine guidance is much more emphatic. The radiance of Aezanas' conversion shines through this Greek text, whereas it glimmers rather more faintly, if nonetheless unmistakably, in the Ethiopic already quoted.

The problem of Aezanas' representation of himself as a Christian in his capital city is complicated still further by the remarkable fact that the recently discovered stone with the Greek text bore on its other side an inscription in Ge'ez that is terminated along a side edge of the block.[12] There are many puzzles about this new Ethiopic inscription, not least because it does not reproduce the content of the Greek text and is written in the fancy Sabaic *musnad* script with South Arabian *mimation*, but exceptionally from left to right. It looks as if this stone had been fitted into the side of the throne that was being dedicated, and this has led the editors of the Ethiopic text to assume that the Greek, with its fulsome acknowledgment of Christ and the Trinity, must represent a missing opening section of the Ethiopic text, but if so we have to ask where those opening lines could have been inscribed. All that we have starts at the top of the stone, and so conceivably any missing lines stood on another block that formed the other side of the throne.

But that would be a desperate solution. The Ethiopic as we can read it actually refers to the Lord God (*'gzbḥrm*) and the Lord of Heaven (*'gz'm śmym*), and the extension of the text on the side ends terminates at the bottom with a highly visible Christian cross.[13] Even so this block remains problematic, with its different texts in different languages, including the alien Sabaic script, for the Ge'ez, written oddly, as if in Ethiopic script, from left to right. The Christianity of the *negus* is plain, but it would seem as if he had not fully moved beyond the ambivalence he felt in publicizing it when he confined himself in his other inscription to expressing gratitude only to the Lord of Heaven, who made his kingdom and the earth beneath it.

Whether the new faith of Aezanas should be ascribed to the missionary work of Frumentius remains an open and insoluble question. The story of the conversion of Ethiopia at the hands of a bishop of that name remains a familiar one to historians of the early Church. But his arrival in Axum after a pirate raid off the coast and his reported connections with Athanasius in Alexandria are much too imprecise and ill documented to verify. It is at least clear that the Byzantine emperor himself, the Arian Constantius, was unhappy to have a disciple of the orthodox Athanasius, who had been driven repeatedly into exile, as his Christian missionary to the Ethiopians. We have seen that this emerges clearly from Constantius' complaint in the letter that Athanasius himself cited in 356. Frumentius' mission could easily be located in the years before that, when Aezanas made his first professions of Christianity on both inscriptions and coins.

A considerably later throne inscription, clearly modeled on the throne texts of Aezanas, comes from his successor Ella Asbeha, known as Kālēb. This text shows a fully developed Christian preamble in Ge'ez, once again in Sabaic script: "To the glory of the Father, the Son, and the Holy Ghost."[14] By the early sixth century Christianity had undoubtedly put down strong roots in Axum. Ares and Maḥrem were gone forever, even though Ella Asbeha (Kālēb) chose to maintain both local and foreign scripts in which to proclaim his faith at Axum, exactly as his great predecessor had done.

Among the rulers between Aezanas and Kālēb, however, there had been another Christian *negus*, whose coin legends serve to explain the transition across the long period from Aezanas in the late fourth century to Kālēb in the sixth. He is a mysterious ruler known only from coins, including one magnificent gold specimen.[15] His name appears as MḤDYS, but since the vocalization is unknown there is no way of telling how this name would have looked with vowels. The coin has no Greek equivalent. It is clear that he ruled in the early 450s. The legends on the coins leave no doubt that he took the lead, immediately after the Council of Chalcedon of 451, in placing his nation squarely among the Monophysites in the Christian East. After the Chalcedonian affirmation of the inseparability of Christ's two natures, human and divine, in one person, those who adhered to belief in his single divine nature—Monophysites—had broken away to form a substantial population of Christians in the Near East. To emphasize his role, MḤDYS presented himself as a kind of Ethiopian Constantine. Just as Constantine reported seeing the cross in heaven with the promise *in hoc signo vinces* "In this sign (the cross) you will conquer," he announced explicitly through the Ethiopic text on his coinage that he too would conquer by the cross (*masqal*). Ethiopic *temawe'* ("he will conquer") corresponds exactly with *vinces*, and MḤDYS attached the epithet *mawā'ī*, (*victor*) to his name, just as Constantine was *maximus victor* or *victoriosissimus*.[16] In this way he advertised a new era of felicity at the very time he established the Monophysite credentials of his Axumite court.

In laying claim in the sixth century to overseas territories that he did not actually rule, Kālēb not only followed in the tradition of Aezanas whose throne inscriptions he imitated but equally in the Constantinian imperialism that MḤDYS had proclaimed. As these claims became increasingly strident, they were matched by social and political upheavals in Ḥimyar. The irredentism of the Ethiopian monarchy was just as strong as ever, but events across the Red Sea served to provide an incentive for the Axumite regime to realize its ambitions in southwest Arabia by coming to the rescue of persecuted Christians.

Fatefully, just as a religious conversion had emboldened a new leadership in Ethiopia to take on a more aggressive and more public posture, a comparable religious conversion had achieved something similar among the Arabs in Ḥimyar. What happened concomitantly on both sides of the Red Sea reflected the old and the new territorial claims of the two kingdoms. But the religions to which the Ethiopians and the Ḥimyarites converted were not the same. Their conversions ultimately struck the spark that ignited an international conflagration.

6

JUDAISM COMES TO ḤIMYAR

The history of southwest Arabia has largely been written from its inscriptions. They are abundant and detailed, and they help to fill the chronological gap in the documentary record that extends from the second inscription on the Adulis throne, with its account of the first Ethiopian conquests in the peninsula, down to the departure of the Ethiopians from Arabia, for reasons that are still unknown, about three-quarters of a century later.[1] If the arrival of the Axumite armies can be placed no later than the early third century, under the leadership of a king called Gadara, or just possibly Sembrouthes, as argued previously, the presence of these invaders is no longer visible from about 270 onwards. Conceivably the Ethiopian withdrawal was the result of negotiation because no violent conflict is attested, but by the time of Aezanas in the middle of the fourth century the memory of rule in Ḥimyar was, as we have seen, sufficiently vivid to move him to arrogate such titles as King of Ḥimyar, Saba, dhū-Raydān, Tihāma, and Ḥaḍramawt. This was a considerably more audacious claim than that made by his early predecessor in the fragmentary Greek inscriptions at Axum and Meroë referring to Ḥimyarites and Axumites,[2] and it was infinitely more mendacious. Aezanas was clearly laying claim to the territories from which his people had withdrawn at the end of the previous century.

In Ḥimyar itself this claim did not go unnoticed. From the reign of the Ḥimyarite king Abīkarib 'Asad—from the first half of the fourth century onwards—a very similar repertoire of titulature begins to appear on the Sabaic inscriptions of the kings of Ḥimyar. Abīkarib himself, as the full form of his titles reveals, boasted that he was King of Saba, dhū-Raydān, Ḥaḍramawt, Yemen, as well as of the Arab tribes of Tawd ("high country"), and Tihāma (on the coast).[3] The last two items were added by the year 440 to titles that his predecessors had already assumed. Such an explosion of imperialist titulature in both Ethiopia and Ḥimyar over a fifty-year period from the later fourth century to the early fifth, with the Ethiopians starting first, can hardly be coincidental. The Ḥimyarites must have become aware, either from traders' reports or from actual visits, of what their former overlords were asserting in Axum, boldly making audacious claims in their own Sabaic script and, at least in part, through their language (with the use of *mimation* and some vocabulary).

Just as reports of the territorial boasts of the *negus* reached the Arabian peninsula, news of his conversion from paganism to monotheism must have arrived there as well. Of course South Arabia had encountered monotheism before through its various Jewish communities, particularly those that had settled in the Ḥaḍramawt. A fourth-century synagogue has now been identified in the port city of Qana' on the southern coast of Yemen,[4] and a traveling Indian evangelist called Theophilus reported on the Jewish communities he encountered in the region when he was sent to convert the Ḥimyarites in the fourth century.[5] Furthermore, the ancient Jewish tribes in Yathrib (the future Medina) in northwest Arabia would have been known in the South through commercial contacts along the trade routes for spice and incense. The Jews of Yathrib were thought in some traditions to be descended from emigrants fleeing from Palestine after Vespasian's devastation of Jerusalem in the first century AD.[6] So the monotheism that sprang up in Axum would certainly not have been incomprehensible to the Ḥimyarites, even if they lacked any deep understanding of either Christian doctrine or Christian sectarianism. They knew monotheism when they saw it, because they had had a long experience of polytheism, just as the Ethiopians had. The pagan Arab pantheon was extensive, allegedly including some 360 divinities,[7] but with some, like Hubal in the northwest and Raydān in the southwest, more prominent than others.

On the other side of the Red Sea monotheism in Ethiopia was breaking up its ancestral paganism. The worship of Maḥrem (Ares in Greek) yielded to the Christian God, even as the rulers in Axum proudly proclaimed their new faith, just as they had in pagan times, in Sabaic script alongside Ethiopic and Greek. More significantly, the Ethiopians also came to see themselves, by a process that is still not well understood, as descended from Solomon through a legendary union with the Queen of Sheba, despite the awkward fact that the kingdom of Sheba (Saba) lay in the south of the Arabian peninsula. Nonetheless, the Ethiopians found no difficulty in claiming descent from the House of David without ever considering themselves Jews. This paradox of Ethiopian Christianity has lasted to the present time and is memorably enshrined in Ethiopia's national book, the *Kebra Nagast* ("The Glory of Kings").[8] The Ark of the Covenant was (and still is) believed to reside in Axum, destined to return to Jerusalem only with the Second Coming.

The legendary origin of the Ethiopian people had, therefore, through the Queen of Sheba, a mysterious and ill-defined connection with the Arabs of the peninsula and with the Jews who resided in it. The basic story is narrated in the *Kebra Nagast* and devolves from a report that an Ethiopian merchant of a certain Queen Makeda brought back from Jerusalem. He had allegedly accepted an invitation from King Solomon to the merchants of the world to bring him exotic treasures for which he promised to pay generously in silver and gold. This merchant brought back such extravagant tales of Solomon's wisdom and magnificence that the queen decided to go herself to meet him. By a ruse he succeeded in sleeping with her and fathering a child called Menelik, whom Solomon eventually anointed king of Ethiopia and the founder of a dynasty there. It was Menelik who surreptitiously took the Ark of the Covenant from the temple in Jerusalem and conveyed it by raft to Ethiopia.[9]

This bizarre narrative involves the Queen of Sheba because Makeda was obviously identified with the biblical Queen who went to hear the wisdom of Solomon. This queen, whose visit to Jerusalem is described in the first *Book of Kings* of the Hebrew Bible, has often been identified with the "Queen of the South," who appears in the New Testament in a similar mission to Solomon. Although the land of Sheba was undoubtedly Saba in southern Arabia, the Septuagint's correct rendering of the name as Saba in Greek might readily have been misunderstood, through an easy confusion of vowels, with Seba, which was the name of one of the sons of Kush, himself the son of Ham and the Semitic eponym of the Ethiopians (Kushites). Hence Sheba could be imagined to lie in East Africa, and that is exactly where Josephus, in the first century AD, put it when he called it the royal capital of Ethiopia. The queen Kandake, whose eunuch meets Philip in the *Acts of the Apostles*, came, in the Christian tradition, to be seen as the very queen who slept with Solomon and generated the royal line of Ethiopia. It seems clear from this Christian text as well as the nearly contemporaneous report of Josephus that by the early Roman Empire the link between Jews and the Ethiopians had already spread widely enough in the Near East to make its appearance in both Jewish and Christian literature at almost the same time.[10] Kandake's name looks very much like a deformation of the Ethiopian name Makeda that appears in the *Kebra Nagast*, although a less plausible connection with Macedonia has sometimes been invoked because of Ethiopian legends concerning Alexander the Great. Whatever the etymology, there can be no doubt that Makeda is the *Kebra Nagast*'s Queen of Sheba.

The Christianity of the Ethiopians was further complicated by their refusal to accept the dyaphysite orthodoxy decreed at the Council of Chalcedon in 451. In the *Kebra Nagast* the emperor Marcianus, who presided over that council, is denounced as an apostate. The Ethiopians' steadfast support of Christ's one nature inevitably brought them close to the Monophysite communities of Syria and Palestine and alienated them from Byzantium. But, as time went on, it was to become clear that geopolitical imperatives could nevertheless bring these two Christ-loving nations together when necessary, despite their doctrinal differences.

It can hardly be an accident that precisely when these momentous changes were happening in Ethiopia the kings of Ḥimyar, who had taken over all the grandiose titles of the Ethiopian kings, suddenly and remarkably also became monotheists. But their monotheism was authentically Jewish and bore no visible connection with the mythology involving the Queen of Sheba that grew up in Axum. This extraordinary development in Arabia, so closely following in time the changes in Ethiopia, is amply documented in the Sabaic epigraphy. As Christian Julien Robin, the leading authority on Ḥimyarite inscriptions, has emphatically asserted, from 380 onwards polytheism utterly vanished from South Arabia.[11] The disappearance of polytheism there and the appearance of imperialist royal titulature occurred in roughly the same period.

In the first four centuries of the Christian era 800 inscriptions, according to Robin's count, document the many gods of South Arabia's pagan temples. But after 380 there is not one pagan text out of approximately 120 documents between 380 and 560. The accretion of monotheist inscriptions led scholars at first to a cautious hypothesis that the peoples of the region had merely acquired a murky and ill-defined taste for monotheism without taking it seriously. Such muddled religiosity was thought to have reflected the confusion of Jewish and Christian perspectives in the world that encompassed them. But with the addition of more detailed documents it has become absolutely certain that the Arabs of Ḥimyar genuinely embraced Judaism as converts. This is not so much apparent from their use of Hebrew on inscriptions as from the introduction of such unambiguous language for themselves as "the people of Israel." Although God appears sometimes simply as "the Merciful (*Rahmanān*)," he is also explicitly invoked as the "Lord of the Jews," and persons with Jewish names are found imposing burial regulations designed to segregate Jews from non-Jews. Occasionally the divinity is called vaguely "Lord of Heaven and Earth," much as he was in the earliest, less overtly Christian inscription of Aezanas at Axum.[12]

A confluence of monotheist ideas in the region seems inescapable, even if one stream flowed towards Christ and the other towards Yahweh. The Ḥimyarites took over such words as Amen and Shalom, and a Ḥimyarite seal, now in a private collection, bears a representation of a menorah with a name in Sabaic letters. The presence of Ḥimyarites (Greek *Homêritai*) in a tomb at Beth She'arim in Palestine may reflect the rise of Judaism in later fourth-century Ḥimyar,[13] or it may simply indicate Jews who traveled there from some of the early local communities such as Theophilus had observed. The same can be said of the Jewish girl Leah, whose bilingual epitaph, in both Hebrew and Sabaic, turned up in the vicinity of Jerusalem.[14]

Whatever uncertainty exists in interpreting the evidence for Jewish Ḥimyarites in Palestine, none exists when it comes to Judaism as the religion of the government in Ḥimyar in the fifth and early sixth centuries. The epigraphical evidence is amply reinforced by literary traditions that concern two notorious episodes of coercion and brutality on the part of the Arab Jewish kings in their dealings with Christian communities in the kingdom.

The first episode, from the third quarter of the fifth century concerns a Christian martyr called Azqīr, known to us from an Ethiopic synaxarion (church calendar), which makes explicit reference to rabbis who assembled in judgment on him.[15] He was put to death in his own city, Najrān, and afterwards some thirty-eight other Christians were reportedly martyred, including priests, monks, and bishops. The second episode is known from a rich dossier on the massacre of Christians in 523 carried out at Najrān by a Ḥimyarite king whose full name was Yūsuf As'ar Yath'ar, sometimes simply called Joseph in modern literature.[16] Because of the notoriety of his anti-Christian pogrom he appears repeatedly in ancient and medieval texts, and under various nicknames—dhū Nuwās ("long-haired") in Arabic, Dounaas (apparently a form of the Arabic name) in Greek, Masrūq ("the comber" perhaps alluding to torture) in Syriac, and Finḥas (the Biblical Phineas) in Ethiopic.[17] The episodes of both Azqīr and the Najrān martyrs constitute incontestable evidence for the persecution of Christians by their Jewish overlords, and both reveal concerted efforts to force conversion to Judaism.

The Judaism of the government in Ḥimyar in the fifth and early sixth centuries has become by now, after more than a century of doubt and uncertainty, an acknowledged fact of Arabian history. The rich epigraphical evidence is amply reinforced by the literary traditions for the two brutal episodes of coercion and brutality. But the massacre at Najrān is by far the more important of the two persecutions that the Jewish regime in Ḥimyar launched against the Christians within their kingdom. It not only convulsed but transformed central and southwestern Arabia. It provoked an invasion from Ethiopia that installed Christianity as the official religion of the kingdom for nearly fifty years, and it allowed not only the *negus* in Axum but the emperor in Constantinople as well as the king of Sassanian Persia to confront one another indirectly in this remote region by intervening in the politics and the religion of the Arabian peninsula. This, in turn, positioned all three rulers to become power-brokers in the rapidly changing world into which Muḥammad was born, in about 570 according to the Muslim tradition enshrined in the Prophet's biography (*sira*). The Arab pagans never lost sight of the traditional polytheist culture that the conversion of the Ḥimyarites to Judaism had seriously curtailed, and the Ka'ba at Mecca preserved memories of Hubal, to whom that ancient sacred monument was thought to have been once dedicated. Furthermore, the presence of newly energized Christian communities that owed their salvation to the monotheist Ethiopians guaranteed that the Persians would have to work hard to reassert their traditional alliances with both Jews in Arabia and the Naṣrid rulers (the so-called Lakhmids) just north of Arabia at al Ḥīra. The sheikhs of al Ḥīra had long been Persian clients who were opposed to Byzantium's Arab clients at Jabala to the northwest—the Jafnids (often called Ghassānids).[18] The tumultuous events in sixth-century Arabia may reasonably be called the crucible of Islam.

It was the pogrom at Najrān in 523 that portentously inaugurated the challenge to the old order. Fortunately we need no longer speak with uncertainty about the date of the massacre, since recent research by Robin and his student, Iwona Gajda, have finally established 110 BC as the chronological era that was used in the Ḥimyarite dating that appears in the epigraphy.[19] We can now date with confidence those texts that display numbers of the Ḥimyarite era, and, on the basis of the inscriptions that Gajda and Robin have analyzed, we can say that after a brief restoration of Ethiopian-sponsored Christianity in Ḥimyar somewhere between 518 and 522, the militantly Jewish Yūsuf revived the Judaism that had dominated the kingdom ever since the end of the fourth century.

The irredentist claims of Axum that had begun with Aezanas at almost the same time as Judaism came to Ḥimyar had grown ever more strident as the monarchy in East Africa became more Christian. Ella Asbeha, the strong *negus* who assumed the biblical name of Kālēb, can be observed through his inscriptions to have been an advocate not only of Ethiopia's claims to territory in the Arabian peninsula but no less of its extraordinary claim to represent the house of David and to boast direct descent from Solomon. His Ge'ez inscriptions leave no doubt about the Solomonic origins that the Ethiopian monarchy espoused. They quote the Bible, particularly the Psalms, and they proclaim the glory of David.[20] So when the Jewish king of Ḥimyar, Yūsuf, reasserted Jewish rule in Ḥimyar in about 522, Kālēb was already poised to invade the country, in fact for the second time. We know from the surviving list of chapter headings for the lost parts of the Syriac *Book of the Ḥimyarites* that he had launched a campaign in Arabia a few years earlier,[21] and this campaign seems clearly to have led to the short-lived Christian occupation of Arabia in the years just before 522.

Our knowledge of Yūsuf's aggressive assault against the Christians inside his own kingdom depends upon a complex dossier of interrelated texts, in which the massacre at Najrān is the principal and recurring theme. These include, first and foremost, the Greek hagiographical account (*martyrion*) of the martyrdom of Ḥārith, or St. Arethas as he is known in Greek, at Najrān as well as the horrific letter written in Syriac by a Monophysite priest (or perhaps bishop) called Symeon from Beth Arsham near Seleuceia on the Tigris, inside Persia. There is little doubt that the Greek text of the *martyrion* derives substantially from the letter of Symeon, and that both were written down soon after the events they relate. Symeon's letter was subsequently abbreviated in other Syriac ecclesiastical works. In 1971 Irfān Shahîd was able to publish a second letter about the Najrān massacre and argued that this was yet another text by the same Symeon of Beth Arsham.[22] A very recent stylistic analysis of these two letters by David Taylor in Oxford has, however, shown conclusively that the second letter is not only not by the author of the first but of far less historical value.[23] Neither letter, as he insists, should be treated as a straightforward historical document because both are obviously tendentious, even though the first is full of details that look genuine. They can, to some extent, be controlled by another Syriac work, the fragmentary *Book of the Ḥimyarites,* but that is no warrant for assuming, as Shahîd did, that Symeon was also the author of that too.

What emerges from these texts is that Yūsuf tried to wipe out the Christian churches in his kingdom either by destroying them or turning them into synagogues, and by trying to force their communicants to convert to Judaism. One of the documents gives a horrifying account of his pledge of safety to those who surrendered to him at Ẓaphār, only to have his forces kill three hundred of them in custody and set fire to a church where another two hundred had congregated. He concentrated his efforts on the significant Christian population of Najrān. He himself reported on his persecution in a letter that he sent to a meeting held at Ramla, southeast of the Naṣrid camp at al Ḥīra, under the auspices of sheikh al Mundhir (Alamoundaros in Greek) together with the support and representation of his ally, the Persian king. The Byzantine emperor Justin also sent a delegate called Abramios to this meeting, as we know from an account of a later embassy written by his son, Nonnosus.[24] And present of course for the discussions and clearly taking careful notes was Symeon of Beth Arsham, who wrote an account of all that was said. This he dispatched to the homonymous abbot, Symeon, at Gabboula in the Jafnid territory of Syria.

The conference at Ramla thus brought together representatives of both Persian and Byzantine interests, under the auspices of a Persian client, to hear the Ḥimyarite king proudly describe his murderous assault on the Christians of Najrān.

This so incensed Symeon of Beth Arsham that he sounded an alarm for Christians, or at least Monophysite Christians, all over the Near East. He wanted his account of what he heard to be spread to Ethiopia, Antioch, Tarsus, Edessa, and Cappadocian Caesarea. Such activism was fully consistent with what we know of Symeon of Beth Arsham, of whom John of Ephesus wrote, "As if God made him ready and as if the earth had vomited him up, Symeon would suddenly spring up and be present there, since from the greatness of his zeal and fervor of his will he did not rest and sit still in one district."[25] It is hard to imagine how he managed to be in attendance at Ramla, but his presence was obviously in character.

In his letter to the Ramla gathering Yūsuf had described in excruciating detail the torments he inflicted upon the Christians of Najrān. The messenger that read out his letter felt free to supplement it with additional sanguinary details, and amazingly the letter itself incorporated impassioned speeches by some of the martyrs. Why Yūsuf chose to boast of his murderous actions in this way, before the representatives of Byzantium and Persia and in the presence of a dynamic and vociferous Christian, may only be surmised. The Persians had thrown their support behind the Jews in Arabia as well as behind the sheikh, al Mundhir, who hosted the conference. Yūsuf may have wanted not only to win Persian approval for his extermination of Ḥimyarite Christians but, at the same, to have secured a buffer against reprisals from Christian powers such as Byzantium or Ethiopia.

In the case of Byzantium he need hardly have worried at this stage, since the Chalcedonian court at Constantinople showed little interest in coming to the aid of overseas Monophysites. But the irredentist ambitions of Kālēb to recover Ethiopian rule in Arabia were something else. The Ethiopians had a past history of invasion and occupation of the peninsula, and Yūsuf's appeal at Ramla could do nothing to protect him against Kālēb. The massacre occurred in 523, the meeting at Ramla in 524, and Kālēb's army was in Ḥimyar by 525.

7

THE ETHIOPIAN INVASION OF 525

If Cosmas can be trusted in reporting that he was present at Adulis twenty-five years before he was writing, he was there in 523 or 524, precisely the years in which Symeon of Beth Arsham was doing his best to arouse support for the persecuted Christians in Ḥimyar after the pogrom at Najrān. It is therefore of the greatest interest that Cosmas reports that the Ethiopian *negus,* Ella Asbeha (Kālēb) was planning at that moment an overseas campaign against the Ḥimyarites. This can hardly be a coincidence. After all, it was Symeon's intention to summon help for the surviving Christians in Arabia. What is particularly telling in Cosmas' report is that Kālēb ordered the inscriptions on the Adulis throne and stele to be copied at that very time for his personal reference, and this suggests that he saw his forthcoming invasion in the context of earlier Axumite expeditions overseas.

The most recent of these expeditions had been, as we have seen, Kālēb's own just five or six years before. In that expedition he installed a Christian king in Ḥimyar, Ma'dīkarib Ya'fur. The background for this invasion in about 518 helps to explain the violence that broke out at Najrān in 523, and it needs to be looked at carefully. It has become apparent in recent years that Kālēb's first intervention in Arabia was not an effort to subvert the Jewish monarchy in Ḥimyar, which had begun over a century before, but to reinforce a Christian presence that had somehow managed to supplant the Jewish rulers and assume control of the country in the early sixth century. Arabian inscriptions reveal a king called Marthad'ilān Yanūf in Ḥimyar between 504 and 509. There is no explicit evidence that he was Christian, but if he is identical with the Marthad, son of Abdkulāl, this might be inferred from the reported Christianity of his father Abdkulāl in Arabic sources. But such a tenuous inference is immensely strengthened by an intriguing fragment from the Byzantine chronicler John Diakrinomenos, who is cited in the *Ecclesiastical History* of Theodoros Anagnostes.[1]

The fragment states that the Ḥimyarites, who are described as a client nation of the Persians and dwelling in the extreme south of Arabia, had been Jews from the beginning (*anekathen* in Greek) when the Queen of the South, who can be understood here, as in the New Testament, to be the biblical Queen of Sheba, went to visit King Solomon. This startling information shows yet again how the Queen's visit to Jerusalem figured no less significantly in the Arabian tradition than in the Ethiopian, and it indicates a belief, however indefensible, that some Jews had been in the peninsula for a very long time, even before the expulsion from Palestine under Vespasian. John Diakrinomenos clearly believes that the Ḥimyarites had not only been Jews from time immemorial but were still Jews in the early sixth century, since the reigning emperor is identified as Anastasius. The chronicler states that it was in his reign that the Ḥimyarites became Christian, and that they requested a bishop. In a separate fragment he gives the bishop's name as Silvanus. Inasmuch as the dates on the inscriptions of Marthad'ilān Yanūf (504 and 509) fall comfortably within the reign of Anastasius (491–518), the testimony of John Diakrinomenos seems entirely credible when assessed together with the Arabic reports about the king's father.

Marthad'ilān Yanūf's successor appears to have been precisely the man whom Kālēb set up as king in the aftermath of his first invasion of Arabia in ca. 518, Ma'dīkarib Ya'fur. And that was the person whom the fanatically Jewish Yūsuf As'ar Yath'ar (Joseph) succeeded, as he said himself in the letter he sent to the Council at Ramla in 523, as quoted by Symeon of Beth Arsham: "The king that the Ethiopians put in charge of our country has died, and winter has come. The Ethiopians were unable to come against us, and I have taken power throughout the country of the Ḥimyarites."

All this means that the first invasion of Ethiopian forces in the sixth century was not designed to replace a Jewish king with a Christian one but in fact to reinforce a Christian presence that had been there for more than a decade. It is not impossible that the Christians at this time had been suffering some kind of persecution, as the surviving chapter summary in the *Book of the Ḥimyarites* appears to suggest,[2] but if so this could only imply subversive Jewish activities against the relatively new Christian regime. Confessional solidarity would undoubtedly have impelled the *negus* at Axum to undertake this campaign, but the irredentism that had been at the core of Ethiopian foreign policy since the late third century must have been equally decisive. He wasted no time in boasting of his achievements even before readying the forces that he called together once Yūsuf's massacres at Najrān and elsewhere became known.

Kālēb publicly commemorated his first invasion of Arabia at Axum on an inscription in Ge'ez in the South Arabian *musnad* script,[3] clearly in imitation of the inscriptions that Aezanas had so conspicuously set up in Axum more than a century before with his bold, if empty, claims to sovereignty in southwest Arabia. Kālēb's text about the first occupation of Ḥimyar identified his commander as a certain Ḥayyān, and it is thanks to the reappearance of this man's name in the Syriac *Book of the Ḥimyarites* as Ḥyōnā in the context of that very expedition that we can be sure that the inscription refers to it.[4] Kālēb's text proudly asserts, "I built a shrine in Ḥimyar at 'QN'L, zealous for the name of the Son of God, in Whom I believe, and I built His Gabaz and sanctified it by the power of God." The location of the shrine in Ḥimyar has been tentatively identified with the port of Okelis, near the straits of Bāb el Mandab, although the correlation between the name in Ethiopic and the Greek name Okelis cannot be considered definitive, and some pious wordplay may be suspected in the word QN['Y] "zealous" that follows the toponym 'QN'L. What Gabaz or Gabaza (GBZ in the Ethiopic) was and where Kālēb built it is not perfectly clear, but it would appear to be the cathedral in Axum, which is known to have born this epithet, meaning "guardian" or "protector."[5] The text of the inscription refers to "His [God's] Gabaz," and this would only make sense as a reference to a great sacred building. We have already observed that Gabaza is also the name of the actual port where ships anchored in the Gulf of Zula for commerce that came through Adulis, although as a toponym this name would reflect the sense of "custodian."

The governor at Adulis had presumably provided the *negus* with information about the texts that could be read on the ancient throne at the site. This information must have piqued Kālēb's curiosity to the point of ordering copies of the inscriptions to be made for him. His order will have followed the public inscriptions commemorating his first expedition to Arabia and reflected his awareness of the horrors that Yūsuf was by then inflicting upon the Christians in his kingdom.

Although Kālēb may be presumed to have had his own expansionist reasons for launching the invasion in 525 in support of the Ḥimyarite Christians, the Greek narrative of the martyrdom of Arethas provides a full account of the diplomacy that led up to it as well as the details of the expedition across the Red Sea. Justin, the emperor at Byzantium at the time, asked Timothy, the archbishop of Alexandria, to intercede with the Ethiopian ruler to take action, and Justin even addressed a letter of his own to him. He observed that the

Ḥimyarite king had put to the sword the Christians of Najrān, which, he points out, included not only Ethiopians but also Romans (meaning Byzantines) and Persians. Justin urged Kālēb, by the Holy Trinity, "to go forth, whether by sea or by land, against the abominable and criminal Jew." He offered to supply troops of his own that he proposed to bring to East Africa for the purpose. He desired and anticipated complete annihilation and anathema for the Ḥimyarite ruler.[6]

The author of the martyrology of Arethas appears to have had available many logistical details about the fleet that assembled for crossing the Red Sea. A force of 120,000 men was to be transported in ships from the coast of East Africa as well as from Aila (modern Aqaba) in the northern extremity of the Red Sea at the head of the Gulf of Aqaba. A contingent from Barbaria, which evidently meant Somalia, perished on the way to the launching of the expedition. The ships were assembled at Gabaza, glossed in the *martyrium*, as we have already seen, as an anchorage in the Gulf of Zula on the territory of Adulis. The map that has been transmitted in three manuscripts of Cosmas clearly indicates that the place known as Gabaza was located directly on the water of the Gulf of Zula. So the *negus* went up to Adulis and thence to the anchorage at Gabaza to lead his armada of seventy ships to the southwestern part of the Arabian peninsula.

The coast of Arabia directly opposite the Gulf of Zula is full of reefs and unsuitable for a naval landing. So the armada presumably went somewhat towards the south on the coast. The *martyrium* of Arethas reports that Yūsuf and his Ḥimyarites built an iron chain, kept afloat by wooden planks, to prevent the Ethiopians from landing.[7] Remarkably, this chain also figures in three South Arabian inscriptions, in which it is called the chain of MDBN, a name that is assumed to indicate its location. The letters are customarily rendered as Maddabān and are seen as cognate with Mandab, which is the well-known name of the closest point of contact between East Africa and Arabia in the southern part of the Red Sea. Obviously the chain cannot have been placed across the strait that is now called Bāb al Mandab, because it would have made no sense to block north-south traffic. But a barrier to access on the coast close by, possibly at Shaykh Saʿīd, has found favor with many scholars. A thirteenth-century Arab writer, Ibn al-Mujāwir, citing a writer from the eleventh century, reports that when the Ethiopians came to invade Arabia with cavalry and infantry the Arabs stretched out a chain to block them.[8] Whatever this chain was like and wherever it was placed, it was prominent enough to leave enduring traces both in the inscriptions of that time as well as in the later Arabic literary tradition.

The success of Kālēb's second invasion of Arabia was celebrated by the *negus* himself in a great inscription of which substantial fragments survive. It refers to the port (*marsa*) in which he arrived, although the name that followed has unfortunately been lost, and to the help of God in bringing him to shore—conceivably after finding a way through the chain. He boasts that he killed the king of Ḥimyar and burned the palace of Saba.[9] The inscription with its celebration of Ethiopian victories in Arabia is extraordinary in many ways. First, it was not set up in Axum or indeed anywhere in East Africa,

Figure 4. The entire stele containing the inscription in figure 3. This stele displays texts in Greek, Ge'ez in Sabaic script, and Ge'ez in unvocalized Ethiopic script. Photo courtesy of Finbarr Barry Flood.

as the records of Kālēb's earlier involvement in Ḥimyar and the campaigns of his predecessors had been. It was set up in the Arabian peninsula itself, at Mārib, a great city of South Arabia. Second, it was inscribed not in the Sabaic language of the region but in classical Ethiopic (Ge'ez) with a fully vocalized script that is read, unlike the languages in Arabia, from left to right.

So here in the Sabaean heartland we see Kālēb boasting of his conquests in the conquered land itself, and in his own language and script. Conceivably this text was meant for the edification of those Ethiopian Christians who remained behind when the *negus* had returned to Axum. Kālēb's choice of language and script is a startling reversal of the policy of both Aezanas and of Kālēb himself when they had set up their inscriptions in Axum. There, in addition to Greek, the Ethiopic was written in the *musnad* script of South Arabia from right to left. It has never been clear just how many residents of Axum could have actually read these inscriptions, although they would certainly have impressed merchants and other visitors from the Arabian peninsula. But Kālēb used Ethiopic script for his own language when it appeared on his coinage (*Fig.* 5).

Kālēb's Mārib inscription is extraordinary in yet a third aspect. It is studded with biblical references, including a Gospel text. The fragments of the stone show an unmistakable echo of *Matthew* 6. 33 in the surviving words "seek first the righteousness" and "will be added to you." Although these phrases imply a slightly different textual tradition from the texts of the Ge'ez Bible, they are clearly based on "Seek ye first

Figure 5. A gold coin of the Christian Axumite king Ousanas in the second half of the fifth century AD. He appears with a turret-crown on the obverse, and, on the reverse, the headcloth traditionally associated with Ethiopian kings. The legends are in Greek on either side of a cross, with King Ousanas named on the obverse and "the grace of God" on the reverse. Nothing is known of this king beyond his coinage, but it influenced the issues and self-representation of Kālēb, who added Ethiopic script. Images courtesy of the American Numismatic Society, where the coin is 1973. 108.2 in the Islamic cabinet.

the kingdom of God, and his righteousness; and all these things shall be added unto you."[10] There are also notable citations from the Psalter. *Psalms* 67 [68]: 1 is invoked to show that God put Kālēb's enemies to flight. The biblical text is "Let God arise, let His enemies be scattered," for which the inscription fragment gives, "As the Psalm says, 'He will rise up. . . . [ene]mies before him.'" Equally arresting are other paraphrases from the *Psalms*. For example, *Psalms* 65 [66]:17 reads "I cried unto Him with my mouth, and He was extolled with my tongue." On the Mārib stone we find "I cried to Him with my mouth and shouted to Him with my tongue." At another point we can see the language of *Psalms* 19 [20]: 7–8: "Some trust in chariots, and some in horses, but we will remember the name of the Lord our God. They are brought down and fallen. But we are risen, and stand upright." The text of the inscription gives something very close to this: "Now they have horses and chariots, while we will be great by the name of God our Lord; they have stumbled and fallen but we have risen. . . ." To what extent these remarkable allusions and near-quotations inform us about the date of the earliest Ethiopic translations of the Bible remains an open question, but they leave no doubt whatever about Kālēb's representation of himself as carrying out his mission in Arabia under biblical authority.

Another passage in the Mārib text seems to provide a striking example of the legend of Ethiopia's descent from the union of Solomon and the Queen of Sheba, as it is fully told in the *Kebra Nagast*. Kālēb makes claim to "the glory of David" (*kebra dāwīt*). This epigraphic allusion to the house of David finds an echo in the literary text of the Arethas *martyrium*, when Timothy of Alexandria is said to have joined with a crowd of Egyptian monks in urging Kālēb to lead an expedition to Ḥimyar. The author of the narrative declares that Timothy urged him to go forth, "just as Samuel had urged David against Amalek."[11] Of course the biblical tradition (*I Kings [I Samuel]* 15:17–18) has Samuel sending Saul against the Amalekites, not David, but the error in the *martyrium* is a telling indication of the reliability and probable contemporaneity of the *martyrium*'s source. It reflects Kālēb's own presentation of himself as a new David in the inscription at Mārib.

Other parts of the Mārib stones with Kālēb's triumphalist text about the invasion survived into modern times but have regrettably been destroyed. Even so, the fragments that we have afford a precious glimpse into the religious justification for the expedition of 525 in fulfillment of the long simmering irredentist ambitions of Axum. The biblical tone of Kālēb's inscription accords well with his mission of avenging the deaths of many Christians at Najrān and of assuring the security of a new generation of Christians who would reside in Arabia.

The building or restoration of churches in Ḥimyar was undoubtedly a part of Kālēb's mission during the period of settlement after his victory and before his withdrawal and the designation of a certain Sumyafa Ashwaʿ as his chosen king—the man whose name Procopius hellenized as Esimphaios.[12] Regrettably, much of the testimony for Kālēb's building policy occurs in a late and highly unreliable source, the life of St. Gregentius, a nonexistent saint, who cannot be taken so seriously as some scholars are inclined to do.[13] But there is no doubt that the Ethiopians built one or more churches in addition to the one provisionally ascribed to Okelis during the first expedition to Arabia. In his letter to Ramla, as we have it from Symeon of Beth Arsham, Yūsuf had reported that the Ethiopians had boasted of building a church "in our country" and that he had converted it into a synagogue after killing the Christians who were guarding it.[14] The new letter that has been ascribed to Symeon opens with the sanguinary details about Yūsuf's attack on the Ethiopian church in Ẓaphār, and it includes an account of the murder of three hundred Ethiopian Christians and the burning of their church.[15] Such a horrendous episode from a general persecution that is best known for the massacre at Najrān finds confirmation in three South

Arabian inscriptions that document a massacre of Christians at Ẓaphār and the destruction of churches there in 523.[16] There can be no doubt, therefore, that the Ethiopians had built at least one church in Ẓaphār during their first invasion, and, since the ecclesiastical historian Philostorgius knew of a church in that city that Theophilus of India had built in the fourth century, the Ethiopian one in the sixth century might possibly have been a restoration.[17] This was clearly the building that Yūsuf attacked in 523. According to the *martyrium* of Arethas, Kālēb built a church at Ẓaphār after his defeat of Yūsuf,[18] and we may suspect that this was another restoration of the previously restored church that had been demolished only two years before. The building and destruction of churches were palpable manifestations of the Christian and Jewish powers that confronted each other in Ḥimyar between 518 and 525.

Two other buildings at Ẓaphār ascribed to Kālēb in the life of St. Gregentius (ch. 9) are beyond identification or credibility. Nevertheless, we are fortunate that so much of the surviving evidence for Najrān and Ḥimyar is early, from the middle of the sixth century, and it is manifestly in close touch with the events themselves. New excavations at Ẓaphār led by Paul Yule, who has pioneered the archaeology of late antique Yemen, may eventually provide a clearer picture of what was happening there in the first half of the sixth century.[19]

Whether or not Kālēb himself retired to live in a monastery after he returned from Arabia remains an open question. The final chapter of the *martyrium* reports as much, and there are no documentary references to him after this, whether epigraphic or numismatic. Still less is there any proof that he sent his royal crown to Jerusalem to be displayed on the front of the Church of the Holy Sepulchre, although the *martyrium* reports that he did that too. What is clear, both from Procopius and the Ḥimyarite inscriptions, is that the king he installed in Ḥimyar when he withdrew was soon overthrown by other Ethiopian Christians who had remained in the region. Their revolt raised up a new and powerful Christian ruler who would be the last great Ethiopian king in Arabia.

8

ENTRY OF THE GREAT POWERS

With the disappearance of Kālēb from the historical record, and the brutal and rapid removal of his nominee, Sumyafa Ashwaʿ (Esimphaios) in Arabia, a power vacuum allowed the international role of the great powers of the eastern Mediterranean to become far greater than it ever had been before. Justin had encouraged and supported, with both ships and troops, the Ethiopian invasion of Ḥimyar in 525, but, at least to judge from the rich and nearly contemporary sources that we have examined, this intervention was directly connected with the persecution that the Christians in Arabia had suffered at the hands of Yūsuf. But when Kālēb returned to Axum after his triumph over the Jewish king in Arabia, the relations between the nations on either side of the Red Sea acquired a distinctly more fluid and less confrontational character that could readily accommodate intervention from outside states. This allowed the Byzantine and Persian empires to expand their diplomatic activity in the Arabian territory substantially beyond the traditional client arrangements that had enabled them to exert indirect influence in the past.

It was at this highly sensitive juncture that Byzantium, under its new emperor Justinian, who succeeded Justin in 527, began to play an active role by exploiting the re-established presence of Christians in Ḥimyar to oppose their Persian enemies. His plan was to enlist the support of the Ethiopians. The Ethiopian invasion and occupation of Arabia had certainly not begun as the first step in a proxy war. Both confessional allegiance and irredentist ambitions more than account for Ethiopian militarism at that time. But by the early 530s this militarism had taken on the additional baggage of Byzantine foreign policy, even as Ḥimyar itself was transformed into an overseas territory within the international orbit of Axum. Procopius could not be more explicit about Justinian's aims in dealing with the new balance of power in the Red Sea countries: "The emperor Justinian," he wrote, "had the idea of allying himself with the Ethiopians and the Ḥimyarites, in order to work against the Persians."[1]

The Ethiopian–Byzantine alliance was inevitably uneasy, since the Monophysites were not naturally comfortable with the Chalcedonians. But Justinian seems to have detected an opportunity to intercept Persian commercial interests in the Red Sea by preempting the Persians in buying silk from India that arrived at Red Sea ports. This may well have been the primary motivation for Justinian's surprising subjugation of an ancient Jewish settlement on the small island of Iotabê at the southern end of the Gulf of Aqaba,[2] and it seems equally to have been part of the reason for new diplomatic initiatives launched from Constantinople. But the larger objective of building a power base in Arabia against Persia can be seen in the earliest diplomatic negotiations between Constantinople, Axum, and Ḥimyar, and as these negotiations developed this objective becomes increasingly clear. But it would be naive to ignore the economic incentive that can be observed at Iotabê.

Justinian dispatched two embassies during the brief reign of Sumyafa Ashwaʿ in order to further his program for an Ethiopian-Ḥimyarite alliance with Byzantium against Persia. A certain Julianus led the first embassy, and at about the same time, or a little later, the much better known Nonnosus led the second. This Nonnosus, who acted for Justinian, was the son of Justin's ambassador to Ramla, Abramos, and the grandson of Anastasius' ambassador to the Ḥujrid sheikh Ḥārith of Kinda.[3] He thus represented the third generation of a family entrusted with Byzantine foreign policy in Arabia, and he presumably had good credentials not only through his education but also through the Semitic background of his family. He must have had a good knowledge of one or more Semitic languages and was thus able to communicate, to some degree, with Arab sheikhs. His Greek from Constantinople would have stood him in good stead at Axum, but his fluency in one or more Semitic tongues, if not necessarily Geʿez, would have helped. Nonnosus' father, Abramos, had not only been to Ramla but had subsequently returned to the region soon afterwards, this time on behalf of Justinian, to negotiate a peace treaty with the current Ḥujrid sheikh, Qays or, as he is known in Greek sources, Kaïsos. Like Ḥārith, who had presumably died, Kaïsos ruled over the tribes of Kinda and Ma'add in central Arabia.[4] Abramos not only persuaded him to accept the treaty but even to send his son Mu'awiyya as a hostage to Constantinople to secure it.

These events provide the immediate background to the mission of Abramos' son Nonnosus in about 530. Justinian gave him a twofold charge—to bring Qays back to the capital city and to go himself to Ethiopia to meet the *negus,* who was still Kālēb near the end of his public career. The ever observant Nonnosus entered Ethiopia through Adulis and journeyed from there overland to Axum, taking notes all along the way about what he saw, including the herds of elephants in the vicinity of Aua that he encountered halfway between Adulis and Axum. He left behind a vivid description of his meeting with the *negus,* whose ring he had to kiss after prostrating himself before him.[5] When the great man stood to receive Nonnosus, he was largely nude, wearing only a loincloth together with a pearl-encrusted shawl over his shoulders and belly, bracelets on his arms, a golden turban with four tassels on each side, and a golden torque on his neck. In the company of his courtiers he stood astride a spectacular gold-leafed palanquin mounted on the circular saddles of four elephants that had been yoked together.

An astonishing miniature image of an identical royal pavillion on four elephants has survived in a medieval manuscript to illustrate Kubalai Khan's reception of Marco Polo (*Fig.* 6).[6] This single image furnishes the only extant parallel to

Figure 6. Marco Polo's reception by Kublai Khan in a pavillion on top of four elephants. This image from a manuscript in Paris exactly replicates the scene described by Nonnosus when the *negus* at Axum received him there ca. 530. These are the only known reports of a royal pavillion of this kind, and the great distance in space and time between the two events in which they appear preclude any direct connection, but ancient traditions in both places may have had some common link. Image reproduced from L. Oeconomos, *Byzantion* 20 (1950), 177–178, with plate 1.

the scene that Nonnosus described. It is astonishing for its similarity to the palanquin at Axum. It is even more astonishing because the two royal receptions, held in an artificial chamber mounted on the backs of four elephants, occurred so far apart in time and space, in thirteenth-century Mongolia and in sixth-century Ethiopia.

Unfortunately, despite his intrepid travels and sharp observations, Nonnosus failed to bring back Qays in person to Justinian. Accordingly, the emperor then dispatched Abramos to Arabia for a second time to do just that. Qays finally agreed to go to Constantinople as well as to relinquish his power in central Arabia to his brothers 'Amr and Yazīd, who would guarantee the Byzantine alliance with Kinda and Ma'add. In Constantinople Justinian showed his gratitude for this accommodation by conferring upon Qays a phylarchate over the three provinces of Palestine. That was a momentous step. It constituted the beginning of Byzantine-sponsored Arab control in the region, which continued under Abū Karib, whom Justinian appointed as a provincial governor called a phylarch (tribal chieftain) from the Jafnid (Ghassānid) tribe in Syria. Abū Karib was the son of the great sheikh Ḥārith of Jabala. He received his Palestinian phylarchate, probably within the larger jurisdiction assigned to Qays, as a reward for giving Justinian a tract of extensive palm groves somewhere in northwestern Arabia, in a region known as Phoinikon—worthless, according to Procopius,[7] but useful nonetheless for securing the Byzantine–Jafnid alliance.

It was not long after the exotic spectacle that Nonnosus had so carefully watched at the court of Axum that the victorious Kālēb supposedly retreated to a saintly life in a monastery and sent his crown to Jerusalem to be displayed in the Church of the Holy Sepulchre. Among the Ethiopians who had remained in Ḥimyar after the departure of Kālēb in the expectation of a prosperous life in a new land was the son of a Christian slave from Adulis. His name was Abraha, and his father had been a Byzantine merchant working in the Ethiopian port city. When it soon became clear that the Ethiopians in Arabia were dissatisfied with Esimphaios, they found a sympathetic champion in Abraha, and so they overthrew Esimphaios, locked him up, and installed Abraha in his place as king. Having grown up in Adulis, Abraha would have had ample opportunity to mark the aspirations of Ethiopian kings through observing their many inscribed votive thrones and boastful inscriptions. It is perhaps not surprising that he and his supporters wanted to distance themselves from the court at Axum while remaining in their new Arabian environment. It looks as if Abraha and those who raised him up intended to create a state that was independent of the one that had taken them to Arabia. Such independence sent shock waves through the Byzantine empire, and these dislocations were not lost upon the Persian king. Nor were they lost upon those Jews who remained in the peninsula, above all in Yathrib—the future Medina—where, according to the later Arabic tradition, they had been for many centuries.

Procopius reports that before his retirement Kālēb made two desperate attempts to have Abraha removed from Ḥimyar, but they evidently failed. In his first effort to remove Abraha, he sent over to Ḥimyar a force of three thousand men, but these troops were so beguiled by the landscape and climate of southwest Arabia that they made terms with Abraha and refused to go back home. In his second attempt Kālēb sent troops that Abraha was able easily to defeat. Once he had consolidated his position in Ḥimyar, Abraha understandably fostered a conspicuous independence from the Ethiopian monarchy by making plain that he was unwilling to be, or to be seen to be, a puppet of Axum. The great inscription (*Fig.* 7) that Abraha set up in 547 to immortalize the achievements of his first decades betrays a noticeable coolness towards the *negus* in Axum, who is scarcely mentioned.[8]

Figure 7. The great inscription of Abraha from Mārib, recording the repair of the dam and the international conference convoked there in 547–8: *CIH* 541. Mārib, Yemen. Photo courtesy of Christian Julien Robin.

It is from that inscription we learn that while Abraha was occupied at that moment in major repairs to a ruptured dam in Mārib he had taken advantage of his prominence in Arabia to convoke an international conference. This was undoubtedly the most significant gathering of this kind in the region since al Mundhir had convoked the pivotal meeting at Ramla during the catastrophic reign of Yūsuf. Abraha, as the established Christian monarch of Ḥimyar, had imitated the building policy of Kālēb and constructed or restored churches at both Mārib and at San'a. In convoking his conference of 547 in the context of conspicuous munificence in repairing the dam, Abraha not only asserted his authority as the region's most powerful ruler and as a Christian, but at the same time he implicitly recognized the competing interests of external great powers in the affairs of the peninsula. At Mārib he received ambassadors from the emperor in Constantinople, from the king of the Persians, from the Naṣrid sheikh al Mundhir in al Ḥīra, from the Jafnid sheikh Ḥārith ibn Jabala, from Abū Karib, whom Justinian had by now personally appointed as the phylarch of Palestine, and from the *negus* in Ethiopia, now demoted to only one among many great powers. Abraha clearly recognized, as we can see from the inscription of 547, that his kingdom could simultaneously exploit and influence the ambitions of the main players in the Near East. These were Byzantium (reinforced by Ḥārith), Persia (reinforced by al Mundhir), and inevitably Ethiopia.[9]

But the pagan, or polytheist, Arabs of the peninsula were conspicuous by their absence from the conference at Mārib, although they probably had no single community that could have possibly represented them. With their many divinities they had nothing to hold them together. Even the well established Jewish tribes at Yathrib had no political influence to match that of the delegates to Mārib in 547, and they were counterbalanced at Yathrib itself by strong pagan tribes. The contending religions at Yathrib ultimately joined together in famously receiving Muḥammad when he made his emigration (*hijra*) from Mecca to Medina—which became the new name, meaning simply "city," for the oasis of Yathrib.

In view of what happened later, the pagans and Jews, of whom so little is actually known in the middle of the sixth century, should not be forgotten in reflecting on the last decades of Abraha's kingship. They may possibly explain a dramatic, even desperate move that the king made only a few years after the Mārib conference.

In 552 he launched a great expedition into central Arabia, north of Najrān and south of Mecca. An important but difficult inscription, which was discovered at Bir Murayghān and first published in 1951, gives the details of this expedition.[10] It shows that one of Abraha's armies went northeastward into the territory of the Ma'add tribal confederacy, while another went northwestward towards the coast (*Map 2*). This two-pronged assault into the central peninsula is, in fact, the last campaign of Abraha known from epigraphy. It may well have represented an abortive attempt to move into areas of Persian influence, south of the Naṣrid capital at al Ḥīra. If Procopius published his history as late as 555, the campaign could possibly be the one to which the Greek historian refers when he says of Abraha, whom he calls Abramos in Greek, that once his rule was secure he promised Justinian many times to invade the land of Persia (*es gēn tēn Persida*), but "only once did he begin the journey and then immediately withdrew."[11] The land that Abraha invaded was hardly the land of Persia, but it was a land of Persian influence and of potentially threatening religious groups—Jewish and pagan.

Some historians have been sorely tempted to bring the expedition of 552, known from the inscription at Bir Murayghān, into conjunction with a celebrated and sensational legend in the Arabic tradition that is reflected in Sura 105 of the Qur'an (*al fīl*, the elephant). The Arabic tradition reports that Abraha undertook an attack on Mecca itself with the aim of taking possession of the Ka'ba, the holy place of the pagan god Hubal. It was believed that Abraha's forces were led by an elephant, and that, although vastly superior in number, they were miraculously repelled by a flock of birds that pelted them with stones. The tradition also maintained that Abraha's assault on the ancient holy place occurred in the very year of Muḥammad's birth (traditionally fixed about 570). Even today the path over which Abraha's elephant and men are believed to have marched is known in local legend as the Road of the Elephant (*ḍarb al fīl*). Obviously, the expedition of 552 cannot be the same expedition as the legendary one, if we are to credit the coincidence of the year of the elephant (*'Ām al fīl*) with the year of the Prophet's birth.[12] But increasingly scholars and historians have begun to suppose that the Quranic date for the elephant is unreliable, since a famous event such as the Prophet's birth would tend naturally, by a familiar historical evolution, to attract other great events into its proximity. Hence the attack on Mecca should perhaps be seen as spun out of a fabulous retelling of Abraha's final and markedly less sensational mission. This is not to say that it might not also have been intended as a vexation for the Persians in response to pressure from Byzantium. But it certainly brought Abraha into close contact with major centers of paganism and Judaism in central and northwest Arabia.

Whatever the purpose of the expedition of 552, Abraha's retreat marked the beginning of the end of his power. That in turn provided precisely the opportunity for which the Persians had long been waiting. A feckless and brutal son of Abraha, whose name seems to have been, of all things, Axum, presided over the dissolution of the Ethiopian kingdom of Ḥimyar, and his administration was continued by his half-brother Masrūq.[13] It was a Jew by the name of Sayf ibn dhī Yazan who then undertook to drive the Ethiopians out of Arabia, and although various Arab traditions leave the details of his efforts uncertain it seems clear that he first tried unsuccessfully to solicit the support of Justin II at Constantinople. But this was not forthcoming, first because of the Christian alliance between Byzantium and Ethiopia, and, second, because of Byzantium's recognition that the Persians had thrown their support in the past to the Jews, Yūsuf above all.

So Sayf as a Jew ultimately turned to the Persians in the person of Chosroes I, king of the Sassanian Persians, whom he approached through the mediation of Persia's Naṣrid clients at al Ḥīra. Chosroes responded favorably and sent his general Wahrīz with an army that promptly expelled the Ethiopians once and for all.[14] By 575 or so the Axumite presence was gone, and the Persians recognized that Christians of whatever confession remaining in Arabia both inside and outside Ḥimyar were no more trustworthy than the pagans. The expulsion of the Ethiopians created a religious instability that was only held in check by the occupying Persians. The mixture of pagans and Jews in Yathrib as well as the pagan contemporaries (*mushrikūn*) of the young Muḥammad in Mecca constituted a fertile, not to say explosive, middle ground in Arabia between the Byzantine Christian empire, which was allied with Ethiopia, and the Zoroastrian Sassanians.[15]

The Persian ascendancy, which the Arabian Jews understandably welcomed in view of the former Persian backing of their co-religionists in Ḥimyar, had come to the peninsula not long after Muḥammad allegedly first saw the light of day in Mecca—in 570 by the canonical dating. This year was, at least in tradition, nothing less than the Year of the Elephant, even if the real Elephant may have come and gone decades before. One thing is certain. The final phase of the collision of late antiquity's two great empires started in this fateful and unstable period. As Muḥammad grew up to rally his Believers and to make his emigration (*hijra*) to Medina, which was the date-palm oasis at Yathrib with its strong Jewish tribes, the Persians built up their own resources to the point of invading Palestine. In 614 they captured the holy city of Jerusalem, where they killed or expelled Christians even as the Jewish population welcomed them as liberators.[16] No one at that moment could possibly have believed that the Persian empire would be in its death throes only a few decades later and that the Sassanian monarchy itself would be finished by the middle of the seventh century. Meanwhile, the court at Constantinople would be helpless to stop the Believers from moving into Syria and Palestine.

Adulis, where a single abandoned throne had documented the beginnings of this tumultuous history, lapsed back into the obscurity from which it had first emerged nearly a millennium before in the Hellenistic Age. Only the manuscripts of Cosmas Indicopleustes, together with several dozen broken thrones and inscriptions on the ground in Ethiopia today, survive to enlighten us.

9

RECKONING

Although there is no way of telling exactly when Abraha died, we know that the latest inscription to survive from his reign in Arabia is dated to 558, only six years after his expedition towards Mecca in what may or may not have been the Year of the Elephant.[1] His two sons succeeded him for a brief period of no more than five years, and after that, through the intercession of the Jewish Sayf ibn dhī Yazan, the Persians established control over Ḥimyar and held it in the decades that followed. This constituted a profound shift in the power balance both inside and outside the region, not only because of the enmity between Byzantium and Persia but also because of the renewal of Persian support for Arabian Jews. Ethiopia's *negus* was now definitively marginalized in Axum, although the monarchy continued to exist, to engage in limited overseas diplomacy, and to mint coins into the seventh century down to about 640. In view of the differences between the Monophysite Ethiopians and Chalcedonian Byzantines, the two Christian states drifted farther apart. They were no longer in a position to implement Justinian's policy of supporting a Christian kingdom in Ḥimyar so as to reduce the influence of Persia. The collapse of Abraha and his family in Arabia transformed the social and political fabric of South Arabia. Although under Persian domination there was no possibility of a revival of the militant Judaism of Yūsuf from a half-century before, the Jews in Arabia at the end of the sixth century nonetheless had the satisfaction of knowing that their overlord had long been well disposed towards them.

The dissolution of the nexus that bound Ethiopia to Arabia created a volatile situation, for which a reckoning of some kind was bound to follow. The turbulent ports into which Cosmas Indicopleustes had piously sailed in 523 once again became isolated towns on both sides of the Red Sea and were no longer the staging platforms for imperialist and religious aggression. Persian domination in South Arabia did not, however, preclude Byzantine commercial rivalry in the Red Sea itself. Although documentation is slight apart from competition for the silk trade at the island of Iotabê, it seems probable that Byzantium slipped into the narrow vacuum that was now left between the Arabian peninsula and the coast of East Africa. It would not have been easy at the time to calculate the result of all this political, military, and economic upheaval, but some kind of repositioning of the powers and religions in the region clearly lay ahead. Without strong kings in Ethiopia and

Ḥimyar the international arena was left to the struggle between Byzantium and Persia. Yet in the very midst of this arena the embers of the old conflagration between Jews and Christians, which had been ignited by the Jews in Arabia and fanned by the Ethiopians who attacked them, were still burning.

Out of these embers a new religion was born, and it was this that brought a wholly unanticipated, if protracted, resolution of the instability that the elimination of the house of Abraha had created. Neither the Persians nor the Byzantines could have perceived what was coming, and the hostility between the two fluctuated inconclusively in the final years of the sixth century, only to grow again at the beginning of the seventh. Less than a decade after the Persians assumed control over Ḥimyar the emperor Maurice, who became emperor at Constantinople in late 582, undertook to decentralize the administration of the Byzantine empire and even to divide it up among his three sons. At the same time his military and diplomatic initiatives with the Persians proved so successful that the Persian Chosroes II accepted, at least temporarily, the Byzantine hegemony in Palestine and Asia Minor. Maurice himself undertook rebuilding at the Church of the Holy Sepulchre in Jerusalem. Yet in 602 he was removed and executed by the rebel Phocas, and this led to a period of local turbulence that allowed the Persian king to return to a more aggressive policy towards Byzantium.

It was this renewal of Persian hostility that led directly to the capture of Jerusalem itself in 614. As the Christian poet Sophronius wrote afterwards of the Christian citizenry, "When they saw the presence of the Persians together with their friends the Jews, they ran straightaway and closed the city's gates."[2] But their frantic effort was unavailing. This was the greatest disaster to befall Jerusalem from a foreign invader since the reign of Vespasian nearly six centuries earlier, and the ancestors of the Jews who had fled to Arabia at that time, particularly those in Yathrib, would not have missed the parallel. Nor would the Arab tribe of the Quraysh not far away in Mecca, where, since 610 according to the Arabic accounts, the prophet Muḥammad had been receiving revelations from God through the archangel Gabriel.

Muḥammad saw himself as God's Messenger in conveying to others the revelations he received in Mecca, and these were destined to become the so-called Meccan chapters, called suras, in the Qur'ān, the holy book of the new religion. But among the newly converted supporters of Muḥammad, those who were called "Believers" in his divine message, some chose to leave Mecca soon after the Persian capture of Jerusalem.[3] The reason for their exodus is unclear, possibly reflecting some internal divisions among the Believers or, perhaps more plausibly, revealing a fear that the Persian conquests, particularly the fall of Jerusalem, portended a danger to those Arabs who were not their partisans. For whatever reason, families who had accepted Muḥammad as their prophet and as God's Messenger emigrated to the other side of the Red Sea in two successive stages. Remarkably the place they chose for their refuge was Axum in Ethiopia, where they would have seen the great steles erected there by earlier rulers. A magnificent specimen is still standing there today (*Fig. 8*).

Whether or not the Believers who fled did so at the invitation of the Ethiopian *negus* is unknown, but there can be

Figure 8. The great Ethiopian obelisk that is still standing at Axum. Photo courtesy of Werner Forman/Art Resource, NY.

little doubt from the testimony in the Arabic tradition, despite the proliferation of obviously fictional anecdotes, that the *negus* welcomed them.[4] The involvement of Ethiopia in Arabia at precisely this period of Persian triumph seems like an uncanny echo of Ethiopian foreign policy in the previous century. Turning to the great international powers at a time of crisis was a maneuver that Muḥammad himself was later to employ, according to another Arab tradition, when he attempted by correspondence to win over various kings.[5] Whatever the truth of the anecdotal accounts, it seems clear that a considerable number of Muḥammad's followers chose to emigrate to Ethiopia. Many remained a long time, while others soon chose to move on when their prophet did.

In 622, in a world in which Byzantium appeared to be overwhelmed by Persian forces that had advanced by now into Egypt, Muḥammad himself decided to emigrate from Mecca to Yathrib, which now became known henceforth simply as Medina ("the city"). This was his portentous *hijra*, which provided the date from which the Islamic era is still calculated today. It was an emigration that came, perhaps like the departure of his followers to Axum, also in response to an invitation. Certain tribal groups in Medina, who may even have been acting in consequence of clandestine diplomacy from Constantinople and the Jafnid Arab allies of the Byzantine emperor, coalesced to bring in God's Messenger,[6] and at this moment some of those who had made the earlier emigration to Axum, which was itself a kind of proto-*hijra*, elected to make a second one by moving on to Medina. It is not impossible that the Byzantine court, which had passed into the hands of the astute emperor Heraclius at the death of Phocas, had seen an opportunity, along the lines of Justinian's foreign policy, to mobilize Arabs in order to build up support abroad that might weaken Persian authority. Certainly Heraclius would have known that the Jews of Yathrib would have been sympathetic to Persia, and that the pagans there, as well as any who were inclined to accept the new revelations of the Messenger, would have had no such sympathy. Both the *hijra* to Axum of Muḥammad's partisans in Mecca and the subsequent and far more famous *hijra* of Muḥammad himself to Medina, along with his remaining partisans and some of those who were in Ethiopia, would appear to be comparable in reflecting the instability in Mecca and to imply some diplomatic interference in the Arabian peninsula from the great powers that lay outside it. The reappearance of Axum at the time of the revelations to Muḥammad, coming after more some forty years of Ethiopian quiescence, suggests no less.

Muḥammad continued to receive his revelations in Medina, and the longer and more complex suras of the Qur'ān are conventionally called Medinan, to indicate the supposed later date of these texts. It was particularly, although not exclusively, in the Medinan revelations that the Messenger drew attention to the pagan communities of Arabs, with whom the Messenger of a new faith had to contend along with the Jews and Christians in the world around him. These pagans have left their traces in later Arabic tradition not only through the reports of 360 different divinities but through the consecration of the ancient structure called the Ka'ba at Mecca to the pagan god Hubal, whose worship was associated with ceremonies of indeterminate origin. In the Quranic texts the pagan Arabs appear under the controversial name "sharers" (*mushrikūn*), polytheists whose gods shared their cult with other gods.

Building upon Gerald Hawting's detailed examination of idolatry in the Qur'ān, Patricia Crone has attempted to discover the nature and extent of Arab paganism in the time of Muḥammad solely on the basis of the text of the Qur'ān and without reference to the huge tradition of commentary on it.[7] She observes, as Hawting did, that most of the references to idols occur in allusions to the remote past rather than the present, and she claims that this suggests that the idols of the Messenger's own day were "conceptual," not physical. But Hawting had already pointed out one verse (22. 30) that clearly alluded to the present: "Avoid the filth that comes from idols (*awthān*)." Crone dismisses this verse as possibly referring to sacrificial stones (*anṣāb*) rather than idols, even though such a reading would make little sense for an Arabian culture that archaeology has shown to have displayed idols publicly throughout the later phases of the pre-Islamic age. The Qur'ān contains controversial words, such as *ṭāghūt* and *jibt*, which may or may not have designated those idols that were clearly indicated by *aṣnām* and *awthān*, but it contains nothing to imply that when idols were designated unambiguously by those words they were not physical idols but conceptual ones. To deny that they were tangible objects, in a world where idols could be seen in temples and on the ground, is minimalist beyond plausibility or credibility.

Crone observes that idols recur in the Quranic references to Abraham, and this is significant because Abraham himself not only rejected idols but was believed to have been some kind of monotheist. This means that Abraham was undoubtedly a figure of contemporary historical relevance for Muḥammad. The problem of what he meant in the earliest Islamic decades emerges nowhere so vividly as in Sura 3. 67, a Medinan verse for which Crone did not provide an analysis: "Abraham was not a Jew nor a Christian, but he was *ḥanīfan musliman,* and he was not one of the *mushrikūn*." In other words, Abraham was not a pagan ("sharer"), nor was he a Jew or a Christian. What was he then? Presumably some kind of monotheist. He was not a Muslim in the confessional sense, nor could he have been, being an ancient figure from time immemorial. Since we are explicitly told that he belonged to neither of the two monotheist religions before Islam, the possibility of pagan monotheism naturally arises. It would be tempting, in the light of recent arguments for a monotheistic interpretation of some manifestations of Graeco-Roman paganism, to adopt this explanation for Abraham. There was certainly no doubt that the Messenger saw Abraham as his great predecessor, unsullied by the filth of idolatry, and the reference to him as *muslim* in Sura 3. 67 can only be taken in the literal sense of someone who had made peace with God. But how would this be different from a Jew or a Christian? Abraham is simply said to have been a *ḥanīf* who made his peace with God.

Unfortunately no one can say definitively what the meaning of *ḥanīf* is, although it is applied in the Arabic tradition to various monotheists in the period of Muḥammad, including not only some early Muslims who supported him but also others who opposed him. So it obviously will not do to interpret being a *ḥanīf* or professing *ḥanīfiyya*—the correlative belief—as an allusion to Islam or to the prophet's Believers. This interpretation depends upon little more than the approving description of Abraham in the Qur'ān. Yet the word is evidently cognate with the Syriac *ḥanpê* to designate pagans, unbelievers, and apostates. In this sense it passed into modern, particularly Christian, Arabic as *ḥanafī* for pagan, heathen, or idolater, and *ḥanafiyya* for paganism. Because the root meaning of the triliteral verb *ḥ-n-f* is to turn or bend sideways, this could imply turning aside either in the sense of abandoning error or of abandoning truth. Abraham's *ḥanīfiyya* had to have been pagan, to judge from the Quranic sura, but the identification of certain of Muḥammad's opponents as *ḥanīfs*, as demonstrated by Uri Rubin, makes it unlikely that Abraham was imagined as some kind of proto-Believer in the party of Muḥammad.[8]

If the paganism of Abraham was monotheist, which is the only possible explanation of the statement that he was not a Jew, a Christian, or a *mushrik*, then we are left to explain all the acknowledged *mushrikūn* of the Qur'ān. To view them all as monotheists too, as Crone is inclined to do,[9] would make the distinction between them and Abraham meaningless. She is undoubtedly correct in emphasizing the existence of a hierarchy among the divinities of the polytheists and a widespread recognition of Allāh as God above others, but the parallels that have often been invoked with the Highest God (*hypsistos theos*) in the Graeco-Roman world not only illustrate comparable hierarchies of pagan gods with one at the top, but equally a diversity of pagan gods, in which the Highest God is by no means always the same and in which there is sometimes no Highest God at all. This would suggest that some pre-Islamic pagans might have been monotheist, just as Abraham was, but it also suggests that since he is said unambiguously not to have been a *mushrik* it would be unreasonable to assume that there was some sort of different class of *mushrikūn* who were, in fact, monotheists.

Abraham seems to have been a unique case before Muḥammad, or at least this is what the Qur'ān would have us believe. This leaves us with useful testimony about the nature and extent of Arab paganism on the eve of Islam. But it also leaves us with *ḥanīf* in the days of the Prophet. That such people were monotheists can hardly be doubted, but that they were all faithful Believers is certainly in doubt. Turning away from polytheism did not necessarily mean accepting the Messenger's revelation.

The very ambivalence of the term *ḥanīf* encapsulates the reckoning that took place in the aftermath of the struggles between Ethiopia and Arabia in the sixth century. The Quranic assertion that Abraham was neither a Jew nor a Christian, and was not a polytheist (*mushrik*) either, exposes the theological space into which the angel Gabriel propelled God's Messenger through the revelations that began in Mecca and continued in Medina. The paradoxical double sense of the word *ḥanīf* or *ḥanafī*, which allows it to describe both a Believer and a pagan, implies a world in which there could be both true and false monotheisms. The struggles between Jews and Christians had already demonstrated this. But polytheism had to be reckoned in as well, and the dualist Zoroastrianism of the Persians, who worked in consort with the monotheist Jews, showed that there was no inevitable alignment through visions of the godhead. Hence Muḥammad had to steer a course that was as treacherous theologically as it was politically and militarily.

Whether all this means, as several historians, like Hawting and Crone, are now arguing with growing confidence, that the polytheists (*mushrikūn*) in the Qur'ān—the pagans in the time of Muḥammad—were all monotheists may be doubted. This new orthodoxy turns upon the undoubted hierarchy of divinities among the polytheists and claims that if God or Allāh is supreme among the various gods the polytheists have necessarily to be considered monotheists. Although this is a paradox, it is not, in fact, so arresting as it sounds. As we have already observed, pagan divinities throughout antiquity have been assigned ranks in relation to one another. Even those universally acknowledged monotheists, the Jews, recognized at one time in their ancient past an assembly of gods over which God himself presided, and throughout the Graeco-Roman world Zeus and Jupiter clearly had a comparable role to that of the old Jewish God. The translation of the Hebrew Bible into Greek in the corpus that we know as the Septuagint complicated the story by rendering a divine messenger (*mal'āk*) with the Greek word for messenger (*angelos*). This had the fateful consequence that such a being became increasingly known as an angel, a divine mediator between the supreme god and humans or other gods. The appearance of angels made the divine hierarchy more visible, but it was not an innovation. In classical Greece, the paradigmatic messenger of the Olympians, and of Zeus above all, was Hermes. No one called him an angel then or now, but that is precisely what he was.

Hence the currently fashionable claim that all Arab polytheists as they appear in the Qur'ān must really have been monotheists is a conceptual sleight of hand that hardly alters the theological context in which Muḥammad found himself. His monotheism was strict in its affirmation of one God, no less so than the monotheism of the Jews and the Christians. The angels of these monotheists mediated between God and man, but they did not mediate between God and lesser Gods.

As time went by, the cult of saints in Christianity looked more and more like a recreation of the old pagan divine hierarchy, but it was never the same even if it appealed to the insatiable human appetite for a realm of intercessors to provide closer access to God Himself.

Muḥammad must have recognized the risks, and his awareness of Jews and Christians, as revealed in the Medinan suras of the Qur'ān, ought to be seen in the context of his repudiation of the polytheists, not only those he had observed in Mecca before the *hijra* but those still worshipping their various gods and idols elsewhere in Arabia. The upheavals that the conflict between Jewish Ḥimyar and Christian Axum had provoked led, after the end of Ethiopian rule under the surrogate king Abraha and his family, to a markedly more powerful Persian influence in the region than before. This resurgence of Persian control had vastly complicated the pagan Arab world when Muḥammad undertook to change it.[10] What still remains open to speculation is the extent to which his Message would have been different if the tumultuous history of Arabia in the decades before him had also been different. But regrettably that is something we shall never know.

Some scholars have postulated episodes of serious climatic change in Arabia during the sixth century to explain the absence of archaeological testimony in certain regions during this period. This might suggest a lack of productivity or growth that could have made a restive population receptive to Muḥammad's message.[11] But there is simply no way of telling. Even the traveler Cosmas, the man who carefully recorded the existence and inscription of the Adulis Throne, had not the slightest curiosity about the overseas expedition of the *negus* for whom he copied the texts he found on the throne and its adjacent stele. He was writing his book a quarter-century after he had been at Adulis, and by then the destruction of the Jewish kingdom in Ḥimyar was a thing of the past. The Ethiopian Christians were securely planted in its place. But he gives no sign that he knew anything at all about all this or even cared about it. By the time he composed his *Christian Topography* he must have been writing largely from his notes, even though he observed two solar eclipses in 547 and thought them worth mentioning.

Cosmas clearly never went back to Adulis after his visit between 523 and 525, and, so far as we can tell, he never interrogated anyone else who went there. The followers of Muḥammad who went to Ethiopia in the so-called first *hijra* would probably have landed at Adulis on their way to Axum, but like Nonnosus, who also passed that way after Cosmas, they too appear to have left no report of any throne or stele at the site. If neither was there anymore, we can only wonder whether, while retreating to a life of piety, Kālēb himself might have chosen to remove these memorials to predecessors whose exploits he had so brilliantly surpassed. Whatever happened, no one ever mentioned the Throne of Adulis again. Even so, its ghostly presence still casts a long shadow over the whole history of ancient Ethiopia and Arabia on the eve of Islam, and it provides both background and context for the momentous events of that time.

Appendix

NONNOSUS

Three emperors at Constantinople in the early sixth century—Anastasius, Justin, and Justinian—entrusted delicate negotiations in the Red Sea region to members of the same family. One of them, Nonnosus, wrote about his activities in an account available to Photius and took care to place them within the context of the work done by both his grandfather and his father.[1] These civil servants must have been well known and trusted at the Byzantine court, and their embassies, five in all to the Arabian peninsula and one to Ethiopia, imply a high level of competence in the culture and presumably languages of the region. The history of Nonnosus and his family opens up a unique perspective on Byzantine efforts to influence and control Arab tribes in southwestern and central Arabia both directly and indirectly (through the Ethiopians).

Nonnosus' account begins with a brief allusion to a mission led by his grandfather, and then includes more detailed accounts of overlapping missions led by his father and himself. The text that Photius read and summarized was clearly available to Malalas when he wrote his *Chronography* not much later than Nonnosus was writing. Later Theophanes Confessor also had access to Nonnosus' work when he was composing his *Chronography* early in the ninth century. Although Nonnosus does not register the diplomatic events in chronological order, it is possible, despite his somewhat confusing cross-references, to segregate the several embassies comprehensibly.

First, the family. Nonnosus tells us that his father's name was Abramēs.[2] This is a variant of the Greek form of his father's name, Abramios, in the *Martyrium of Arethas* §27. The name, but not the person, also appears in Procopius as Abramos for a king of Ḥimyar we know as Abraha.[3] This name may be rendered as Abraham, as indeed it appears in Syriac precisely with reference to Nonnosus' father.[4] It is obviously Semitic. Whether it means, as Müller thought when he prepared the Nonnosus *testimonia* for his *Fragmenta Historicorum Graecorum*, that Nonnosus was a Syrian may be doubted. But a near eastern origin is likely. In view of the missions in which this family was involved, it would be reasonable to assume that the family was not only Arab but conversant with sixth-century Arabic, then in its formative period,[5] and perhaps Sabaic and Syriac as well. All these languages would have been useful for ambassadors to the Arabian peninsula. Since Nonnosus himself, unlike his father and grandfather, was also dispatched to Axum in Ethiopia, where he was formally received by the *negus*, who received him while standing in a royal pavillion on top of four elephants,[6] it is possible that this diplomat of the third generation had taken the trouble to master Ge'ez, the classical Ethiopic language of the Axumite court, which is itself another Semitic language. Familiarity with local cultures was nothing new in the appointment of governors and military officers throughout the Roman and Byzantine empires, but a diplomatic specialization across three generations of one family was most unusual.

Nonnosus reports that the emperor Anastasius had sent his grandfather on an embassy to the Arab phylarch Arethas (Ḥārith), with whom he concluded a peace treaty. There can be little doubt that this is the peace treaty assigned by Theophanes to the year 502/3: "Anastasius made a treaty with Arethas, the father of Badicharimos and Ogaros. . . ." For the previous year Theophanes recorded a broad Arab invasion into Phoenicia, Syria, and Palestine when Badicharimos launched a fierce campaign after the death of his brother Ogaros (Ḥujr). How or where Ogaros died is beyond knowing, but the devastation that Badicharmos wrought understandably attracted the attention of Constantinople,[7] not least because about the same time (502) the Persian Shah, Kawad, revoked a treaty between Persia and Byzantium that had been in effect for more than half a century. Ḥārith, the father and phylarch, was the Ḥujrid ruler of Kinda in central Arabia,[8] and he had to take account of his Arab enemies, the pro-Persian Naṣrids of al-Ḥīra, who would have been responsive to Kawad's decision to renew hostility against Byzantium. He would therefore have been disposed to make a settlement with the Byzantines after the Ḥujrid invasion of Palestine.

Anastasius acted at once and dispatched an expert, Nonnosus's grandfather, who, as we know from a later Syriac source, bore the name Euphrasius.[9] So far as can be told from Photius, Nonnosus did not even mention his grandfather's name, but it points to Mesopotamia, and perhaps an origin for the family not far removed from al-Hīra itself and the Arabian peninsula. In view of the success of Euphrasius' embassy, it seems that Anastasius chose well.

With this background from 502 it is hardly surprising that Nonnosus' father, Abraham, was dispatched by Justin to ransom two Byzantine *duces* whom the forces of the Naṣrid sheikh al Mundhir had captured along with their soldiers. Procopius reports that these two officers were Timostratus, brother of Rufinus, and John, son of Lucas.[10] Nonnosus names them both as the *duces* (he calls them *stratêgoi*) who were the prisoners of war whom his father managed to recover by paying, according to Procopius, an extravagant ransom. Abraham went subsequently with al Mundhir southeast of al-Hīra to participate in a conference that the sheikh convened in 524 at Ramla. It may be that this was not far from the homeland of Abraham's family, descended from Euphrasius, since we already know that another of the delegates to that conference, Symeon of Beth Arsham, definitely came from southern Mesopotamia.[11] Hence Abraham and Symeon may have spoken to one another in the same language, Syriac or Arabic, or possibly both.

There is no way of telling where al Mundhir's forces had captured the two *duces*, but the narrative in Procopius implies that it was somewhere in central or northern Arabia, where none of the Byzantine officers or client phylarchs were strong enough to resist them.[12] Relations between al-Ḥīra and Kinda were inevitably unstable, because Persian support for the Naṣrids had to be balanced against Byzantine support for the Ḥujrids as secured by Euphrasius in 502. Malalas reports that al Mundhir, with a force of 30,000 men, had pursued the Kindites of Ḥārith southwestward into the desert, where he captured and killed "the phylarch of the Romans."[13] It has sometimes been supposed that Abraham's negotiations on behalf of Justin in 524 led to a peace treaty with al Mundhir, but Nonnosus makes no mention of anything other than the recovery of the two prisoners, who, he says explicitly, had been held according to the law or custom (*nomos*) of war. It was during Abraham's next mission to Arabia, early in the reign of Justinian, that he actually did conclude a peace treaty, but this was with the ruler of Kinda, Ḥārith's successor.[14]

At least as far as can be told from Photius' summary, Nonnosus introduced this second embassy of Abraham out of chronological order. Photius explictly states that it had occurred before Nonnosus' own embassy for Justinian, even though that is mentioned first. The confusing structure in the patriarch's summary arises from the appearance of the Kindite phylarch Kaïsos (Arabic Qays) in both missions. The peace treaty that Abraham negotiated provided for the remission of Qays' own son, Mu'awiyya, to Constantinople as a hostage.[15]

Justinian then sent Nonnosus himself to bring Qays to the city as well. He identifies this man as a descendant of Ḥārith, with whom Abraham had negotiated in 502,[16] and he goes on to identify him correctly as a ruler of two Saracen tribes, the Chindenoi and the Maadenoi—precisely the peoples of Kinda and Ma'add in central Arabia. Now that Qays' son was a hostage in Constantinople, Justinian evidently wanted to bring the phylarch himself there. The motivation for this mission is unclear, but it may well have represented an effort to remove a powerful leader who might have been open to solicitation from the Persian side as represented by the Naṣrids. In any case, it is clear from Nonnosus that he failed to bring back Qays, and so Justinian sent his father Abraham back to Arabia to try again.

Abraham succeeded in bringing out Qays and, at the same time, to transfer Qays' phylarchy to his two brothers, Ambros and Iezidos, whose Arabic names were obviously 'Amr and Yazīd. This was a brilliant piece of diplomacy that allowed Justinian to enlarge his influence in Arabia by personally appointing the new rulers of Kinda and Ma'add, which are both explicitly named in Nonnosus' report. In Constantinople Justinian expressed his pleasure with the new arrangements by formally bestowing upon Qays the hegemony (*hêgemonia*) over the three Palestines as well as the tribes that had been subjected to him previously. From Nonnosus' Greek, at least as reported by Photius, there appears to have been a clear administrative hierarchy in which Qays' hegemony ranked above the phylarchies of his brothers, and it included their subjects in Arabia as well as those who resided in the

Palestinian lands.[17] Since Procopius reports that the Jafnid Abūkarib was phylarch of Palestine later in the reign of Justinian, he must have operated under the general hegemony assigned to Qays.[18]

Nonnosus' failed mission to Kinda was but one part of the twofold diplomatic assignment that Justinian had given him. The other had been an embassy to the king (*negus*) of Ethiopia in Axum. Inasmuch as this king is explicitly named in Greek as Elesbaas, we can be sure, from his appearance in comparable Greek renderings (above all in Procopius and the *Martyrium of Arethas*[19]), that he is the *negus* known from inscriptions at Axum as Ella Asbeha, or, as he was generally known, Kālēb,[20] the energetic Christian ruler who launched an invasion of the Arabian peninsula in 525 to wipe out the savage Ḥimyarite monarchy of Arab converts to Judaism.[21]

After his victory over the king, Yūsuf As'ar Yath'ar, Kālēb left behind a contingent of Ethiopian Christians in charge of Ḥimyar under a certain Sumyafa 'Ashwa', whom Procopius knew as Esimphaios. This man was soon overthrown by another Ethiopian Christian in the occupying army, Abraha from Adulis. Despite Kālēb's abortive attempts to remove Abraha,[22] the aging *negus* soon resigned himself to a monastic life of piety.

It must have been between his Arabian victory and his retirement to a monastery that Kālēb received Nonnosus in Axum, a city that Nonnosus calls Auxoumis and Procopius Auxōmis.[23] It is clear from Malalas that Nonnosus took a lively interest in the exotica of the royal ceremony as well as in the memorable scenes he encountered as he made his way from the port town of Adulis to the capital. At Aua, he saw a herd of 5000 elephants grazing in a vast open space that not even the natives found easy to penetrate.[24]

But Nonnosus' visit principally reflected a policy that Justinian had devised in his early years as emperor. This was to strengthen Byzantine opposition to Persia by intervening in Arabian affairs with the help of Ethiopia.[25] Procopius is explicit about Justinian's decision to appeal to the Ethiopian Christians, both those in their native highland of East Africa and those who had been settled in Arabia, to join forces with the Byzantines. The three missions of Nonnosus' father Abraham must therefore be seen in the light of Justinian's effort to gain support in the Red Sea territories.

Joëlle Beaucamp has recently and compellingly argued that this kind of interventionism in the region did not characterize Byzantine foreign policy before Justinian.[26] But there were clearly adumbrations of it in the mission of Euphrasius under Anastasius as well as in Abraham's first mission, which took place under Justin. We can readily accept Procopius' report that Justinian was the first to lobby both the Ethiopians and the Arabs as a means of thwarting the Persians, but there is no doubt that the Persians had themselves been active well before that in supporting the cruel regime of the Jewish rulers of Ḥimyar, whose anti-Christian policies had ultimately led to the pogrom at Najrān. That would not have escaped the notice of Anastasius and Justin. Both emperors, like their successor Justinian, had ample need of the energy and talents of the family of Nonnosus.

TABULAR REPRESENTATION OF THE EMBASSIES OF NONNOSUS' FAMILY

502	Euphrasius, sent by Anastasius to Ḥārith (Arethas) of Kinda and concludes peace treaty.
523/524	Abraham (son of Euphrasius) sent by Justin to al Mundhir at al-Hīra to ransom two captured *duces* and to participate in the conference at Ramla.
ca. 528	Abraham sent by Justinian to Qays (Kaïsos) of Kinda, concludes peace treaty, and arranges for Qays' son, Mu'awiyya, to go to Constantinople.
ca. 530	Nonnosus, Abraham's son, sent by Justinian to Kinda to have Qays himself removed to Constantinople; Nonnosus then sent, as part of the same mission, to Axum to meet the *negus* Ella Asbeha (Kālēb).
ca. 530/531	Abraham sent again by Justinian to Kinda because Nonnosus had failed to remove Qays. Abraham successfully negotiates transfer of Qays to Constantinople and arranges for his brothers, 'Amr and Yazīd, to assume his phylarchy in Arabia.

Notes

Chapter 1

1. Another possibility would be a derivation from the old Egyptian toponym WḌLṮT, cf. G. Fiaccadori, *La parola del passato* 335 (2004), 108 and J.-C. Goyon, *Topoi* 6. 2 (1996), 654. For Littmann's suggestion see the following note.
2. E. Littmann provides a brief summary of the ancient and modern work on Adulis in Pauly-Wissowa's *Realencyclopädie*, Supplementband VII (1940), cols. 1–2, but the best review of the evidence and bibliography is the article on Adulis in the *Encyclopaedia Aethiopica*, vol. 1 (2003), pp. 104–105. See also R. Paribeni, "Richerche sul luogo dell'antica Adulis," *Monumenti Antichi* 17 (1907), 437–572. For an informative account of the short-lived British survey, see David Peacock, Lucy Blue, and Darren Glazier, *The Ancient Red Sea Port of Adulis, Eritrea: Results of the Eritro-British Expedition 2004–2005* (Oxbow Oxford, 2007).

3. *Periplus* 19: a land route from northwest Arabia "to Petra, to Malichus, king of the Nabataeans." On the king's reign, see G. W. Bowersock, *Roman Arabia* (Harvard, 1983), pp. 69–72.
4. *Periplus* 4 in the translation of L. Casson, *The Periplus Maris Erythraei* (Princeton, 1989). On pp. 100–106 and 271 Casson provides a commentary on this passage, with discussion of the claims of Massawa, as well as remarks on the city Ptolemaïs (Ptolemaïs Thêrôn) and the phrase "legal emporium," on which more in the next chapter. I have altered Casson's renderings of "innermost" and "outermost" to reflect the ancient usage of "inner" and "outer" to designate remoteness from a geographical point of reference, here the southern end of the Gulf of Zula. For this usage see chapter 2 below.
5. Casson (preceding note), p. 103, prefers the small islands directly off the coast of Massawa. Yet this identification is hardly necessary.
6. *Mart. Areth.* §29 (*MarAr* p. 263): "a harbor called Gabaza, which is in the territory of the coastal city Adulis." Gabaza appears once more in the *martyrium* (§31, *MarAr* p. 269), on traveling from Adulis to Gabaza.
7. See the report by Peacock and others cited above in note 2. Unfortunately, the name Didôros for the island is consistently misspelled in that report as Diodôros. The British team makes a good case for identifying the otherwise unknown site of Samidi, which appears in Cosmas' drawing, with two mounds north of Adulis that have architectural fragments and large upright stones.
8. *CAC*, p. 42.
9. *RIE* vol. 1, no. 191, l. 36 (p. 273): *gbzh*.
10. Cosmas Indic., *Topogr. Christ.* 2. 54–63.
11. *DAE* vol. 2, pp. 45–69, with *RIE* vol. 1, p. 22.
12. J. Aliquot, *Inscriptions grecques et latines de la Syrie*, vol. 11, Mt. Hermon (Beirut, 2008), p. 32.
13. Details may be found in vol. 1 of Wolska-Conus' 1968 edition of the *Topography* in the *Sources chrétiennes* series: p. 366 for the Adulis drawing and pp. 45–50 on the three manuscripts. I am informed that Maja Kominko will soon publish with the Cambridge University Press a substantial book on Cosmas' work, with a new discussion of the manuscripts and reproduction of the illustrations, which all appear in Wolska-Conus' edition.
14. *DAE* vol. 2, p. 45. See also chapter 5 below for further comment on the remains of Axumite thrones.

15. For *stêlê* in the sense of "statue" in late antiquity see D. Feissel, *Chroniques d'épigraphie byzantine 1987–2004* (Paris, 2006), p. 146 [no. 452] and 360 [no. 1185].
16. Cf. *RIE* vol. 3 A. pp. 26–45, nos. 276 and 277, and *FHN* vol. 3, pp. 948–953, no. 234. English translations of the text of these inscriptions appear in chapters 3 and 4 below.
17. Cosmas Indic., *Topgr. Christ.* 2 56.

Chapter 2

1. Cosmas Indic., *Topogr. Christ.* 2. 54.
2. W. Wolska-Conus, *La topographie chrétienne de Cosmas Indicopleustès* (Paris, 1962, published under the name Wanda Wolska), pp. 1–11, and her introduction to the edition of the *Topogr. Christ.* in the series *Sources chrétiennes*, no. 141, vol. 1 (Paris, 1968), pp. 16–17.
3. Cosmas Indic., *Topogr. Christ.* 2. 30 (Horn of Africa [Barbaria]) and 49 (Ḥimyar).
4. Cosmas Indic., *Topogr. Christ.* 3. 65, "in Taprobanê, an island in inner India."
5. Cf. G. W. Bowersock, with reference to the Syriac life of Rabbula, in *Greek Biography and Panegyric in Late Antiquity*, ed. T. Hägg and P. Rousseau (Berkeley, 2000), p. 266.
6. "Palladius," *De gentibus Indiae et Brahmanibus* 1.
7. *Periplus* 30, "an island . . . called Dioscourides, very big, deserted, and damp, with rivers, crocodiles, many vipers, and enormous lizards." The name Socotra is presumed to be derived from the—*scourid*—element of Dioscourides. Cf. Cosmas Indic., *Topogr. Christ.* 3. 65.
8. See Getzel M. Cohen, *The Hellenistic Settlements in Syria, the Red Sea Basin, and North Africa* (Berkeley, 2006), pp. 325–326. Cosmas Indic., *Topogr. Christ.* 2. 65.
9. Christian Julien Robin and Maria Gorea, "Les vestiges antiques de la grotte de Ḥôq (Suqutra, Yémen)," *CRAI* 2002, pp. 409–445. Other graffiti that appear to be in an Indian language have been entrusted to Mikhail Bukharin, who has also published the first Indian inscription from South Arabia itself: *Qāni' Le port antique du Ḥaḍramawt*, ed. J.-F. Salles and A. Sedov (Turnhout, 2010), pp. 399–401.

10. Cosmas Indic., *Topogr. Christ.* 2. 56 (twenty-five years earlier), 6. 3 (two eclipses).
11. *Periplus* 5, "Zoskales, fussy about his possessions and always enlarging them, but in other respects an excellent person and well acquainted with Greek letters."
12. Pliny, *Nat. Hist.* 6. 34, 174.
13. Pliny, *Nat. Hist.* 6. 31, 141. Cf. D. W. Roller, *The World of Juba II and Kleopatra Selene* (London, 2003), ch. 10 ("On Arabia"), pp. 227–243.
14. Cosmas Indic., *Topogr. Christ.* Prol. 1. Who the Christ-loving Constantine might have been is unknowable, conceivably the Praetorian Prefect of the Orient with that name in the early sixth century (*Prosopography of the Later Roman Empire*, vol. 2 [Cambridge, 1980], p. 315).
15. Cosmas Indic., *Topogr. Christ.* 2. 35–36. Cf. 5. 20–49. Cf. *Epist. Hebr.* 8. 5.
16. Wolska-Conus 1962 (n. 2 above), pp.129–133, "Cosmas n'abonde pas en précisions géométriques" (p. 133). Cf. *Job* 38. 37–38. The cube is invoked at Cosmas, *Topogr. Christ.* 2. 18, with a citation of the Septuagint text of *Job*.
17. Lionel Casson, *The Periplus Maris Erythraei* (Princeton, 1989), pp. 274–276.
18. *Periplus* 4. Cf. H. H. Scullard, *The Elephant in the Greek and Roman World* (London, 1974).

Chapter 3

1. Getzel M. Cohen, *The Hellenistic Settlements in Syria, the Red Sea Basin, and North Africa* (Berkeley, 2006), pp. 338–343 on Philotera and Ptolemaïs. It is suggested that the former was located at Marsa Gawasis and the latter at Aqiq on the coast. M. Bukharin has recently proposed Anfile Bay as the endpoint, mentioned in the *Periplus* 3, from which ships returned to Ptolemaïs of the Hunts to board elephants after sailing southwards along the coast of Eritrea to pick up obsidian: "The Notion *τὸ πέρας τῆς ἀνακομιδῆς* and the Location of Ptolemaïs of the Hunts in the *Periplus of the Erythraean Sea*," *Arabian Archaeology and Epigraphy* 22 (2011), 219–231. See also the survey of Ptolemaic ports on the Red Sea in the introduction to Timothy Power, *The Red Sea from Byzantium to the Caliphate*, AD 500–1000 (Cairo, 2012).

2. For the ivory trade under Augustus, see chapter 2 above. On documentation for the elephant industry in the Ptolemaic period, see the important papers by Lionel Casson, "Ptolemy II and the Hunting of African Elephants," *TAPA* 123 (1993), 247–260, and Stanley Burstein, "Elephants for Ptolemy II: Ptolemaic Policy in Nubia in the Third Century BC," in *Ptolemy II Philadelphus and his World*, ed. P. McKechnie and P. Guillaume, *Mnemosyne* Supplement 300 (Leiden, 2008), pp. 135–147. See the two papyrus documents presented in *FHN* vol. 2, nos. 120 and 121, pp. 572–577, on the organization and payment of elephant hunters.
3. The literature on this bizarre practice is immense and by no means concordant. Cf. Keith Hopkins, "Brother-Sister Marriage in Roman Egypt," *Comparative Studies in Society and History* 22 (1980), 303–354, and Sabine R. Huebner, "Brother-Sister Marriage in Roman Egypt: a Curiosity of Humankind or a Widespread Family Strategy?" *JRS* 97 (2007), 21–49.
4. Cosmas Indic., *Topogr. Christ.* 2. 57: "We found, sculpted on the back of the throne, Heracles and Hermes. My companion, the blessed Menas, said that Heracles was a symbol of power and Hermes of wealth. But I, recalling the *Acts of the Apostles*, objected on one point, saying that it is preferable to consider Hermes a symbol of the *logos*." Cosmas cites *Acts* 14. 12 in support of his view.
5. See the commentary on this inscription in *RIE* vol. 3 A, pp. 26–32, especially p. 30.
6. Herod. 4. 183. 4; Strabo, 16. 4. 17 (p. 776 C).
7. Pliny, *Nat. Hist.* 8. 26.
8. *FHN* II. Nos. 120 (P. Petrie II. 40 a, III 53 g) and 121 (P. Eleph. 28) from 224 and 223 BC respectively. See P. M. Fraser, *Ptolemaic Alexandria* (Oxford, 1972), I, pp. 177, with II, pp. 298–299, note 346.
9. *RIE* III, p. 29 and Fraser, *op. cit.*
10. *Sylloge Inscriptionum Graecarum*, 3rd ed., no. 502.
11. Bert van der Speck and Irving Finkel have placed an invaluable account of the chronicle and related texts in their preliminary study posted on the Internet at http://www.livius.org/cg-cm/chronicles/bchp-ptolemy_iii/bchp_ptolemy_iii_02.html. The papyrus on Ptolemy's reception at Seleuceia is from Gurob in the Fayyum (*FGH* 160). The cuneiform tablet is BM 34428. For these events, see, above all, H. Hauben,

"L'expédition de Ptolémée III en Orient et la sédition domestique de 245 av: J.-C.," *Archiv für Papyrologie* 36 (1990), 29–37.

12. G. W. Bowersock, *Roman Arabia* (Cambridge MA, 1983), pp. 48–49.

Chapter 4

1. *RIE* vol. 1, nos. 269, 270, 270 bis, 286, 286 A (pp. 362, 365, 369, 385, 387).
2. See chapter 2 above.
3. For the coinage, *CAC*.
4. For opinions on the various toponyms and ethnonyms, see the commentaries in *FHN* vol. 3, pp. 952–953 and in *RIE* vol. 3 A, pp. 35–43.
5. For Nonnosus' narrative see the Appendix to the present work.
6. Herod. 2. 29 (Meroë as a great metropolis of Ethiopians).
7. Ibn Khaldûn, *The Muqaddimah,* trans. F. Rosenthal, 2nd ed. (Princeton, 1967), vol. 1, pp. 21–22: "He [an early Yemeni king] gave them the name Berbers when he heard their jargon and asked what that 'barbarah' was."
8. *Periplus* 5.
9. Philostr., *Vit. Apoll.* 6. 1 (Meroë in Ethiopia), 6. 4 (for the etymology).
10. For Syriac apocalyptic, particularly with reference to *Psalms* 68. 31, see G. W. Bowersock, "Helena's Bridle, Ethiopian Christianity, and Syriac Apocalyptic," in *Studia Patristica* vol. 45 (2010), pp. 211–220.
11. Ael. Arist., *To Rome*, Orat. 26 (Keil). 70.
12. Cf. F. Fontanella, *Elio Aristide: A Roma, traduzione e commento* (Pisa, 2007), p. 130.
13. C. Phillips, W. Facey, and F. Villeneuve, "Une inscription latine de l'archipel Farasân (sud de la mer Rouge) et son contexte archéologique et historique," *Arabia* 2 (2004), 143–190, with figs. 63–67, and F. Villeneuve, "Une inscription latine sur l'archipel Farasân, Arabie Séoudite, sud de la mer Rouge," *CRAI* 2004, 419–429.
14. Christian Robin, "La première intervention abyssine en Arabie méridionale," *Proceedings of the Eighth International Conference of Ethiopian Studies* (Addis Ababa, 1989), pp. 157–162.
15. See Robin, note above, p. 152–154 for Gadara as *malik* and comparable Arabian inscriptions with references to *ḥabashat*. For Gadara in Ethiopia (Addi Gelemo in Tigray), *RIE* no. 180, pp. 219–220: *gdr / ngśy / 'ksm.*

16. Cf. J. Desanges, "Toujours Afrique apporte fait nouveau," *Scripta Minora* (Paris, 1999), p. 355: "Une datation à la fin du IIe siècle serait historiquement plus facile à admettre, tout en ménageant la priorité dans ces conquêtes hautement revendiquée par le roi d'Axoum anonyme."
17. Hélène Cuvigny and Christian Robin, "Des Kinaidokolpites dans un ostracon grec du désert oriental (Égypte)," *Topoi* 6 (1996), 697–720.
18. Steph. Byz., *Ethnika* s.v. Zadramē. The capital of the Kinaidocolpitai is said to have been called Zadramē. Stephanus claims to be excerpting the Periplus of Marcianus of Heraclea, whose date as well as the date of the source he was using are both unknown. Cf. Stefano Belfiore (ed.), *Il Geografo e l'Editore: Marciano di Eraclea e I Peripli Antichi* (Rome, 2011) with citation on p. 111.
19. Gianfranco Fiaccadori, "Sembrouthes 'Gran Re' (*DAE* IV 3 = *RIÉth* 275): Per la storia del primo ellenismo aksumita," *La Parola del Passato* 335 (2004), 103–157.
20. M. Bukharin has suggested that Romans may have been involved if it was Gadara who went to Leukê Kômê: *Vestinik Drevneii Istorii* 258 (2006), 3–13, on which see *SEG* 56. 2020.
21. *RIE* vol. 1, no. 269, p. 362.
22. *RIE* vol. 1, no. 286, p. 385, and no. 286 A, p. 387.
23. William Y. Adams, *Nubia. Corridor to Africa* (Princeton, 1984), p. 383.
24. Heliodorus, *Aethiop.* 10. 26.
25. For a discussion of this material, with an argument for the date of the composition of the *Aethiopica*, see G. W. Bowersock, *Fiction as History* (Berkeley, 1994), pp. 149–160.
26. *CAC*, pp. 28–29.
27. *CAC*, pp. 29–30, with plates 3–5 [plate 3 for the gold coin with the crown on obverse].
28. *RIE* vol. 1, nos. 185 and 185 bis (pp. 241–250), no. 186 (pp. 250–254), no. 187 (pp. 255–258), no. 188 (pp. 258–261), no. 270 (pp. 363–367), 270 bis (pp. 367–370).

Chapter 5

1. For the emergence of Ḥimyar in South Arabia see Iwona Gajda, *Le royaume de Ḥimyar à l'époque monothéiste* (Paris, 2009), pp. 35–38.

2. See many references in the epigraphy of the Bosporan kingdoms: *Corpus Inscriptionum Regni Bosporani* (Moscow, 1965), nos. 28 (Pharnaces), 31 (Mithridates), 1048 (Sauromates I). Rhescuporis II and III show "king from ancestor kings, *ek progonôn basileôn*" (nos. 1047 and 53). At Palmyra Herodianus and Odainathus adopted the "king of kings," as discussed by M. Gawlikowski, "Odainat et Hérodien, rois des rois," *Mélanges de l'Université St. Joseph* 60 (2007), 289–311, with presumed imitation of Persian titulature.
3. For the pagan texts with Ares and Maḥrem, see the documents cited in n. 28 at the end of the previous chapter.
4. Rufinus, *Hist. Eccles.* 2. 5. 14, on which see A. Dihle, *Umstrittene Daten* (Cologne, 1965), pp. 36–64 ("Frumentios und Ezana"), and also A. Muravyov, "Pervaya volna khristianizatsii," *Vestnik Drevneii Istorii* 261 (2009), pp. 182–185.
5. Athanas., *Apol.* 29. 31.
6. CAC, p. 32. An excellent summary account of the Christianization of Axum may be found in Garth Fowden, *Empire to Commonwealth: Consequences of Monotheism in Late Antiquity* (Princeton,1993), pp. 109–116, although this came too soon after *RIE* vol. 1 to take account of it and antedates *RIE* vol. 3.
7. *DAE* vol. 2, pp. 45–69.
8. *RIE* vol. 1, no. 185, pp. 241–245 (the two Ethiopic texts), no. 270, pp. 363–367 (Greek), with full bibliography, from Salt onwards, in both places. The sumptuous presentation in *DAE* vol 4., nos. 4, 6, and 7 is still invaluable and incorporates German translations of the three texts in parallel columns.
9. *RIE*. vol. 1, no. 185 bis, pp. 246–250 (Ethiopic), no. 270 bis (Greek), pp. 367–370. *Fig.* 3 shows the upper text in Ge'ez.
10. *RIE* vol. 1, no. 189, pp. 263–267 (vocalized Ethiopic but untranslated; for a German translation and commentary, *DAE* no. 11, with a corrected reading at the end of line 1 in *RIE, loc. cit.*). The Greek inscription is *RIE* vol 1., no. 271, pp. 370–372. For an English rendering of the Greek, *FHN* vol. 3, no. 299, pp. 1100–1103.
11. Procop., *Wars* I. 19. 27–33. Procopius says that before their resettlement on the Nile in lower Nubia the Nobatai were living "in the vicinity of the city Oasis" (*amphi polin Oasin*) but a few lines after that he refers to their being "in the vicinity of the Oasis" (*amphi tên Oasin*). Since there was no

city named Oasis, the reference must be to the region of the greater and lesser oases of the Thebaid (Khargeh and Dakhleh). I suspect that the word *polin* in the first reference is intrusive and should be deleted.

12. *RIE* vol. 1, no. 190, pp. 268–271.
13. See *RIE* vol. 2, plate 125 for the top of the Ethiopic inscription, and plate 128 for the cross at the bottom of the very short lines on the side of the block.
14. *RIE* vol. 1, no. 192, pp. 274–278.
15. S. Munro-Hay, "A New Gold Coin of King MḤDYS of Aksum," *Numismatic Chronicle* 155 (1995), 275–277.
16. See G. W. Bowersock, *Studia Patristica* 45 (2010), 218–219.

Chapter 6

1. See the excellent overview of the historical record in Christian Robin's chapter, "L'antiquité" and, for the epigraphical testimony, his chapter "Langues et écritures" in the catalogue of the 2010 Louvre exhibition, *RdA*, pp. 81–99 and 119–131.
2. *RIE* vol. 1, nos. 269 (pp. 362–363), 286 (pp. 385–386).
3. Christian Robin, "Les Arabes de Ḥimyar, 'des Romains' et des Perses (IIIe—VIe siècles de l'ère chrétienne)," *Semitica et Classica* 1 (2008), 167–202, especially p. 171, and Iwona Gajda, *Le royaume de Ḥimyar à l'époque monothéiste* (Paris, 2009), pp. 47–58.
4. G. W. Bowersock, "The New Greek Inscription from South Yemen," in *Qāni' Le port antique du Ḥaḑramawt entre la Méditerranée, l'Afrique et l'Inde*, Preliminary Reports of the Russian Archaeological Mission to the Republic of Yemen, vol. IV (Turnhout, 2010), pp. 393–396. Cf. the remarks of the excavator, A. Sedov, on p. 380 of the same volume.
5. Gianfranco Fiaccadori, *Teofilo Indiano* (Ravenna, 1992).
6. On Yathrib's Jewish population, Fred M. Donner, *Muhammad and the Believers at the Origins of Islam* (Cambridge MA, 2010), p. 35. For the tradition about exiles from the Vespasianic capture of Jerusalem, see A. Bausi and A. Gori, *Tradizioni orientali del Martirio di Areta* (Florence, 2006), p. 121, with the note on the Ethiopic version of the Martyrium.
7. Toufic Fahd, *Le Panthéon de l'Arabie centrale à la veille de l'Hégire* (Paris, 1968).

8. The best edition of this fundamental work remains that of Carl Bezold, *Kebra Nagast: die Herrlichkeit der Könige*, Abhandlungen der I Kl. der Kön. Akad. d. Wissensch. 23, Bd. I (Munich, 1905), with accompanying German translation. The French translation of G. Colin (Geneva, 2002) is serviceable, but the English version by E. A. Wallis Budge (London, 1922) should be avoided.
9. For a summary account see A. H. M. Jones and Elizabeth Munroe, *A History of Ethiopia* (Oxford, 1966), pp. 14–18.
10. For the Queen of Sheba's visit to Solomon, *I Kings* 10. 1–13, and for the Queen of the South's identical visit to him, *Matth*. 12. 42 and *Luke* 11. 31. See also Josephus., *Ant*. 2. 249 and *Acta Apost*. 8. 27. Cf. G. W. Bowersock, "Helena's Bridle, Ethiopian Christianity, and Syriac Apocalyptic," *Studia Patristica* 45 (2010), 211–220, esp. note 8 on Kandake.
11. Christian Robin, *RdA*, p. 88: "Ce rejet du polythéisme est radical et définitif."
12. For the Jewish inscriptions of South Arabia, see the detailed analysis by Christian Robin, "Ḥimyar et Israël," *CRAI* 2004, pp. 831–908.
13. For the seal see Robin (previous note), pp. 891–892, and for Beth She'arim p. 836.
14. G. W. Nebe and A. Sima, "Die aramäisch / hebräisch / sabäische Grabinschrift der Lea," *Arabian Archaeology and Epigraphy* 15 (2004), 76–83.
15. C. Conti-Rossini, "Un documento sul cristianesimo nello Yemen ai tempi del re Ṣarāḥbīl Yakkuf," *Rendiconti dell' Accademia Nazionale dei Lincei, Classe di Scienze morali, storiche e filologiche*, ser. 5, 19 (1910), pp. 705–750, with the Ethiopic text followed by an Italian translation on pp. 747–750. Cf. A. F. L. Beeston, "The Martyrdom of Azqir," *Proc. Seminar for Arabian Studies* 16 (1985), 5–10, reprinted in *A. F. L. Beeston at The Arabian Seminar and Other Papers*, ed. M. C. A. Macdonald and C. S. Philips (Oxford, 2005), pp. 113–118.
16. Christian Robin, "Joseph, dernier roi de Ḥimyar (de 522 à 525, ou une des années suivantes)," *Jerusalem Studies in Arabic and Islam* 34 (2008), 1–124. See the many papers on Najrān in *Juifs et chrétiens en Arabie aux Ve et VIe siècles: Regards croisés sur les sources*, ed. J. Beaucamp et al. (Paris 2010).
17. See Th. Noeldeke, *Geschichte der Perser und Araber zur Zeit der Sasaniden, aus der arabischen Chronik des Tabari* (Leiden, 1879), pp. 174–175 with n. 1 for the Arabic, with MarAr for the Greek, A. Moberg, *The Book of*

the Ḥimyarites (Lund, 1924) for the Syriac, and A. Bausi with A. Gori, *Tradizioni orientali del Martirio di Areta* (Florence, 2006), for the Ethiopic.

18. Fergus Millar, "Rome's Arab Allies in Late Antiquity. Conceptions and Representations from within the Frontiers of the Empire," in *Commutatio et contentio. Studies in the Late Roman, Sasanian, and Early Islamic Near East in Memory of Zeev Rubin*, ed. H. Börm and J. Wiesehöfer (Düsseldorf 2010), pp. 199–226.
19. See the work by Gajda cited above in n. 3.
20. *RIE* vol. 1, no. 195, stone II., l. 24, p. 287.
21. A. Moberg, *The Book of the Ḥimyarites* (Lund, 1924).
22. Marina Detoraki has meticulously reviewed and documented these sources *MarAr*, pp. 13–43. See also I. Shahîd, *The Martyrs of Najrān* (Brussels, 1971).
23. David G. K. Taylor, "A Stylistic Comparison of the Syriac Ḥimyarite Martyr Texts Attributed to Simeon of Beth Arsham," in *Juifs et chrétiens en Arabie* (cited in n. 16 above), pp. 143–176.
24. See the Appendix to this volume on "Nonnosus," as well as my article, "Nonnosus and Byzantine Diplomacy in Arabia," for the Festschrift in honor of Emilio Gabba, *Rivista Storica Italiana* 124 (2012), 282-290.
25. John of Ephesus included a life of Symeon in his *Lives of the Eastern Saints*: *Patrologia Orientalis* 17, fasc. 1, ed. E. W. Brooks (1923), pp. 137–158. The quotation is on p. 140, which also reveals that Symeon went often to al Ḥīra, converted many of the Arabs there, and persuaded them to build a church.

Chapter 7

1. Cf. Iwona Gajda, *Le royaume de Ḥimyar à l'époque monothéiste* (Paris, 2009), pp. 73–81, with Theod. Anagnost., *Kirchengeschichte* (ed. Hansen 1995), p. 157, with which cf. p. 152.
2. A. Moberg, *The Book of the Himyarites* (Lund, 1924), p. 3b. G. Hatke, in his doctoral thesis, suggests a connection with Jacob of Serūg's reference to persecution of Christians in his letter to the Christians of Ḥimyar: *Africans in Arabia Felix: Axumite Relations with Ḥimyar in the Sixth Century* C.E. (Ph.D. dissertation, Princeton, January 2011)

p. 113. Cf. Jacob Sarugensis, *Epistulae*, ed. Olinder (Louvain, 1952), pp. 87–88.

3. *RIE* vol. 1, no. 191, pp. 271–274.
4. Lines 34–35 of the inscription mentioned in the previous note give the commander's name as Ḥayyān (*ḥyn*), and the surviving summary of the relevant chapter (now lost) in the *Book of the Ḥimyarites* names the commander of the first expedition as Ḥyōnā (*ḥywn'*): A. Moberg, *The Book of the Himyarites* (Lund, 1924), pp. 3 and ci. Cf. Iwona Gajda, *Le royaume de Ḥimyar à l'époque monothéiste* (Paris, 2009), p. 80.
5. A. Dillmann, *Lexicon Linguae Aethiopicae* (Leipzig, 1865), col. 1174.
6. *MarAr* ch. 27, with Detoraki's note 164 on p. 256. Justin's words about the enemy were *kata tou musarou kai paranomou Hebraiou*, and for their annihilation he uses the phrase *eis teleion aphanismon kai anathema*. This was strong language to arouse the Ethiopians to do what they were inclined to do anyway. But they doubtless welcomed military support even from Chalcedonian Christians.
7. *MarAr* § 32.
8. In her book cited in n. 1 above, p. 92, Gajda quotes and discusses the South Arabian inscriptions that mention the chain, and she considers the Arabic testimony on p. 94. Fundamental for modern discussions of the chain of Maddabān is A. F. L. Beeston, "The Chain of al Mandab," in *On Both sides of al Mandab. Ethiopian, South Arabic and Islamic studies presented to Oscar Löfgren on His 90th birthday* (Stockholm, 1989), pp. 1–6.
9. *RIE* vol. 1, no. 195, pp. 284–288. See *Fig.* 4, for the upper fragment. For a South Arabian inscription also mentioning the death of the king of Ḥimyar, see Gajda (n. 1 above), pp. 107–108.
10. I am much indebted to George Hatke, for his meticulous analysis of the biblical allusions in this inscription: *Africans in Arabia Felix: Axumite Relations with Ḥimyar in the Sixth Century C.E.* (Ph.D. dissertation, Princeton, January 2011), pp. 378–382.
11. *MarAr* § 28.
12. On this king, see Gajda (n. 1 above), pp. 112–115. Procopius, *Wars* 1. 20. 3.
13. I. Shahîd, "Byzantium in South Arabia," *Dumbarton Oaks Papers* 33 (1979), pp. 25–94. G. Fiaccadori, "Gregentios in the Land of the Homerites," in A. Berger (ed.), *Life and Works of Saint Gregentios, Archbishop of Taphar* (Berlin, 2006), pp. 48–82.

14. I. Guidi, "La lettera di Simeone vescovo di Beth Arsam," *Rendic. Accad. Lincei* (Ser. 3) 7 (1881), 2 [Syriac].
15. I. Shahîd, *The Martyrs of Najrân* (Brussels, 1971), pp. iii-1v [Syriac].
16. G Ryckmans, *Le Muséon* 66 (1953), nos. 507 and 508, pp. 285–287 and 296–297. A. Jamme, *Sabaean and Hasaean Inscriptions from Saudi Arabia* (Rome, 1966), no. 1028, p. 39.
17. Cf. Philostorgius, *Kirchengeschichte* (ed. Bidez-Winkelmann), 3. 4.
18. *MarAr* § 38.
19. P. Yule, "Ẓaphār. Capital of Himyar," *Archäologische Berichte aus dem Yemen* 11 (2007), 477–548. See also the context provided in P. Yule, *Himyar. Spätantike im Jemen / Late Antique Yemen* (Aichwald, 2007).

Chapter 8

1. Procop., *Wars* I. 19. 1,
2. Procop., *Wars* I. 20. 9, on Justinian's desire to involve the Ethiopians in the silk trade in order to disadvantage the Persians who were profiting from it. Justinian recruited the Ethiopians against the Persians because of their shared religion (*dia to tês doxês homognômon*). Iotabê (Procop., *Wars* I. 19. 3–4) was most probably Tiran, although no ancient remains have been discovered there and amphibious landings would have been difficult. On the history and location of the island, P. Mayerson, "The Island of Iotabê in the Byzantine Sources: a Reprise," *BASOR* 287 (1992), 1–4.
3. Julianus' embassy: Procop., *Wars* I. 20. 9. For a full account of the family and diplomatic activity of Nonnosus, see the Appendix to the present volume as well as G. W. Bowersock, "Nonnosus and Byzantine Diplomacy in Arabia," *Rivista Storica Italiana* 124 (2012), 282-290. The basic Greek text of Nonnosus may be found in *FHG* IV, pp. 178–180.
4. Cf. I. Shahîd, "Byzantium and Kinda," *Byzantinische Zeitschrift* 53 (1960), 57–73, and the Appendix below.
5. *FHG* IV, p. 178–180, with the elephants in excerpts preserved in Photius and the meeting with the *negus* in Malalas.
6. L. Oeconomos, "Remarques sur trois passages de trois historiens grecs du Moyen Age," *Byzantion* 20 (1950), 177–183, on Malalas' account of Nonnosus in Axum, 177–178 with plate 1.

7. Procop., *Wars* I. 19. 10–13. Procopius says that Abū Karib was appointed "phylarch of the Saracens in Palestine," by comparison with Nonnosus' description of Qays as receiving "the hegemony of the Palestines [plural]" (*FHG* IV, p. 179).
8. *CIH* no. 541. A good photograph of this impressive stone appears in *RdA*, p. 90.
9. For a comprehensive analysis of Abraha's career in the half century before Muḥammad's birth, see Lawrence Conrad, "Abraha and Muḥammad: Some Observations Apropos of Chronology and Literary *topoi* in the Early Arabic Historical Tradition," *BSOAS* 50 (1987), 225–240.
10. This is the inscription from Bir Mureyghān known as Ryckmans 506, for which see J. Ryckmans, in his article "Inscriptions historiques sabéennes de l'Arabie centrale: Inscription de Muraighān," *Le Muséon* 56 (1953), 339–342, with comment by A. F. L. Beeston, in *BSOAS* 16 (1954), 391–392. A new Murayghān inscription was discovered in 2009 and is still unpublished: cf. Christian Julien Robin in his entry on Arabia and Ethiopia in the *Handbook of Late Antiquity* edited by Scott Johnson (Oxford, 2012), p. 287. It apparently claims that Abraha extended his authority over new territories in northeastern, northern, and northwestern Arabia and asserts that he had expelled the son of the Naṣrid king of al Ḥīra.
11. Procop., *Wars* I. 20. 13.
12. One might also consider another year than 570 for the Prophet's birth: cf. L. Conrad, "Abraha and Muḥammad: Some Observations Apropos of Literary 'Topoi' in the Early Arabic Historical Tradition," *BSOAS* 50 (1987), 225–240, with reflections on the number 40 as a *topos* to explain the interval between 570 for Muḥammad's birth and 610 for the *mab'ath*.
13. Axum appears on an inscription as the king's son *'[k]sm*, CIH 541, ll. 82–83. In Ṭabari he is called Yaksum: Th. Noeldeke, *Geschichte der Perser und Araber zur Zeit der Sasaniden* (Leiden, 1879), p. 219, where a coin with a Greek legend *Iaxômi* is adduced in n. 3.
14. Contemporary or near-contemporary sources for this period are lacking, particularly after the termination of Procopius' *Wars*. For a review of the Arabic tradition and Theophanes, see I. Gajda, *Le royaume de Ḥimyar à l'époque monothéiste* (Paris, 2009), pp. 150–156.
15. For Arab paganism as mentioned in the Qu'rān, see the incisive, but controversial, analysis by Patricia Crone, "The Religion of the Qur'ānic

Pagans: God and the Lesser Deities," *Arabica* 57 (2010), 151–200. Her paper is indebted to the equally controversial thesis of G. R. Hawting's *The Idea of Idolatry and the Emergence of Islam* (Cambridge, 1999), which considers the *kuffār* (non-believers) and *mushrikūn* (sharers) as aberrant monotheists, although they have long been understood to be pagans or polytheists. Both Hawting and Crone believe that these terms express condemnation of certain monotheists by other ones. Crone explicitly examines the Quranic *mushrikūn* without reference to the subsequent tradition—an interesting experiment but arguably not the most fruitful way to handle surviving testimony. Memory, even if corrupted or invented, is important for writing history. Both the Qur'ān and the subsequent tradition clearly acknowledge the existence of many gods before and during the time of Muḥammad. Current debate concentrates, not without circularity, on whether these gods were ranked in a hierarchy with Allāh on top. Even if they were this would be a strange kind of monotheism.

16. On all this see my Jerusalem lectures in memory of Menachem Stern, *Empires in Collision in Late Antiquity* (Hanover, 2012).

Chapter 9

1. Iwona Gajda, *Le Royaume de Ḥimyar à l'époque monothéiste* (Paris, 2009), p. 152.
2. Sophronius, *Anacreont.*, no. 14, ll. 61–64.
3. See F. M. Donner, *Muhammad and the Believers. At the Origins of Islam* (Harvard, 2010).
4. Wim Raven, "Some Early Islamic Texts on the Negus of Abyssinia," *Journal of Semitic Studies* 33 / 2 (1988), 197–218. Irfan Shahîd, "The Hijra (Emigration) of the Early Muslims to Abyssinia: The Byzantine Dimension," in *To Hellinikon: Studies in Honor of Speros Vryonis, Jr.*, ed. J. S. Allen et al., vol. 2 (New Rochelle, 1993), pp. 203–213.
5. Irfan Shahîd, *The Arabs in Late Antiquity: Their Role, Achievement, and Legacy*, American University of Beirut, Jewett Chair of Arabic: Occasional Papers (Beirut, 2008), ed. R. Baalbaki, pp. 27–28.
6. For this suggestion, see M. Lecker, "Were the Ghassānids and the Byzantines behind Muḥammad's hijra?" in the forthcoming publication, ed.

Christian Robin, of the proceedings of a conference on "Cross Perspectives of History and Archaeology on the Jafnid Dynasty" (Paris, 12–13 November 2008).

7. Gerald Hawting, *The Idea of Idolatry and the Emergence of Islam. From Polemic to History* (Cambridge, 1999). Patricia Crone, "The Religion of the Qur'ānic Pagans: God and the Lesser Deities," *Arabica* 57 (2010), 151–200.
8. Uri Rubin, "Ḥanīfiyya and Ka'ba," JSAI 13 (1990), 85–112.
9. But in her paper "Angels versus Humans as Messengers of God," in *Revelation, Literature, and community in Late Antiquity*, ed. P. Townsend and M. Vidas (Tübingen, 2011), pp. 315–336, she regularly refers to the *mushrikūn* as polytheists.
10. For the Persians in this period see now Greg Fisher, *Between Empires: Arabs, Romans, and Sasanians in Late Antiquity* (Oxford, 2011).
11. Cf. Antti Arjava, "The Mystery Cloud of 536 CE in the Mediterranean Sources," *Dumbarton Oaks Papers* 59 (2009), 73–93, and Christian Julien Robin in *Handbook of Late Antiquity*, ed. Scott Johnson (Oxford, 2012), p. 305.

Appendix

1. The surviving texts in Greek, as summarized and paraphrased by Photius, are still most conveniently examined in C. Müller, *FHG* IV, pp. 178–180. The present appendix, is an abbreviated and revised version of a paper in honor of Emilio Gabba in *Rivista Storica Italiana* 124 (2012), 282–290.
2. *PLRE* II. Abramius 2, p. 3.
3. Procop., *Wars* I. 20.
4. Ps. Zacharias, *Hist. Eccles.* VIII. 3.
5. For early pre-Islamic Arabic, see the rich dossier assembled in ed. M. C. A. Macdonald, *The Development of Arabic as a Written Language*, Supplement to the *Proceedings of the Seminar for Arabian Studies* 40 (Oxford, 2010).
6. Müller, *FGH* IV, p. 178. For a picture of a comparable ceremony, L. Oeconomos, "Remarques sur trois passages de trois historiens grecs du Moyen Age," *Byzantion* 20 (1950), 177–183. See *Fig.* 6 in this volume.

7. This must be the devastation by eastern nomads that Procopius of Gaza mentions in his *Panegyric of Anastasius* 7 (pp. 9–10 Chauvot), written between 498 and 502.

8. Cf. I. Kawar (Shahīd), "Byzantium and Kinda," *Byz. Zeitschr.* 53 (1960), 57–73. Id., *Byzantium and the Arabs in the Fifth Century* (Washington DC, 1989), pp. 127–129. Ogaros' Semitic name was Ḥujr, Badicharmos' name was Ma'dīkarib: C. J. Robin, "Les Arabes de Ḥimyar, des 'Romains' et des Perses (IIIe–VIe siècles de l'ère chrétienne)," *Semitica et Classica* 1 (2008), 167–202, particularly 178. It is hard to accept Robin's view (p. 178) that the father of Ḥujr was not Ḥārith, the phylarch of Ḥujrid Kinda, but a hypothetical homonym of the Ghassān.

9. *PLRE* II. Euphrasius 3, p. 425. The name in Greek could, it may be suggested, be analogous to the name Fıratlı in Turkish.

10. Procop., *Wars* I. 17. 44, reprised in Evagr., *HE* IV. 12. Cf. *PLRE* II, p. 1120 (Timostratus), p. 611 (Ioannes 70).

11. David G. K. Taylor, "A Stylistic Comparison of the Syriac Himyarite Martyr Texts," in ed. J. Beaucamp, F. Briquel-Chatonnet, and C. J. Robin, *Juifs et chrétiens en Arabie aux Ve et VIe siècles: Regards croisés sur les sources* (Paris, 2010), pp. 143–176, particularly p. 144. For Ramla, I. Kawar (Shahīd), "The Conference of Ramla," *Journal of Near Eastern Studies* 23 (1964), 115–131.

12. Procop., *Wars* I. 17. 40 (Alamoundaros, Πέρσαις . . . πιστός, plundered the lands from the boundaries of Egypt to Mesopotamia), 46 (neither δοῦκες nor φύλαρχοι could resist).

13. Malalas, *Chron.* 18. 16 (Bonn pp. 434–435).

14. *MarAr* §25 confirms Nonnosus on this treaty.

15. The name of the son is Μαυίας, not Mavia (as in Müller's Latin translation), which would be a woman's name (Arabic Māwiyya), but Mu'awiyya.

16. Robin (n. 8 above) shows that he must have been a grandson.

17. The Greek formulation of the hegemony of Qays is carefully phrased: αὐτὸς τὴν Παλαιστινῶν ἡγεμονίαν παρὰ βασιλέως ἐδέξατο, πλῆθος πολὺ τῶν ὑποτεταγμένων αὐτῷ σὺν αὐτῷ ἐπαγόμενος (*FHG* IV, p. 179).

18. For Abūkarib, Procop., *Wars* I. 19. 10–13, and *P. Petra* IV. 39, l. 165 [ὁ] φύλαρχ[ο]ς Ἄβου Χήρηβος.

19. Procop. *Wars* I. 20. (Hellestheaios). *MarAr* §1, 2, 27, 29, 32, 34 35, 37–39 (Elesbaas).

20. E.g. *RIE* vol. 1., no. 191, pp. 272–273, ll. 7–8, *'n klb 'l ṣbḥ*.
21. This date, like others in this article, reflects 110 BC, which is now agreed to have been the era of Ḥimyar in dated south Arabian inscriptions. See C. J. Robin in n. 8 above.
22. Procop., *Bella* I. 20. 4–7.
23. For Procopius see *Wars* I. 19. 17. Already in the *Periplus of the Red Sea*, from the middle of the first century AD, the Greek form of the city name was *Axōmis, Peripl. Maris Eryth.* 4.
24. See Chapter 4 above.
25. Procop., *Wars* I. 19. 1: "The emperor Justinian had the idea of allying himself with the Ethiopians and the Homerites (Ḥimyarites) in order to work against the Persians." Cf. *Wars* I. 20. 9 on the envoy Julian, whom Justinian sent to Ethiopia and Christian Ḥimyar to join the Byzantines, because of their common religion, to war against the Persians.
26. J. Beaucamp, "Le rôle de Byzance en Mer Rouge sous le règne de Justin: mythe ou réalité?" in Beaucamp et al., eds. *Juifs et chrétiens en Arabie* (n. 11 above), pp. 197–218.

Bibliography

Works in the list of abbreviations are not included here.

Adams, William Y. *Nubia. Corridor to Africa*. Princeton, NJ: Princeton University Press, 1977.

Aliquot, Julien. *Inscriptions grecques et latines de la Syrie*. Vol. 11. Beirut: Mt. Hermon, 2008.

Arjava, Antti. "The Mystery Cloud of 536 CE in the Mediterranean Sources." *Dumbarton Oaks Papers* 59 (2005): 73–93.

Bausi, A., and A. Gori. *Tradizioni orientali del Martirio di Areta*. Florence: Dipartimento di linguistica, Università di Firenze, 2006.

Beaucamp, Joëlle, Françoise Briquel-Chatonnet, and Christian Julien Robin. *Juifs et Chrétiens en Arabie aux Ve et VIe siècles: Regards croisés sur les sources*. Collège de France—CNRS Centre de recherche d'histoire et civilisation de Byzance, Monographies 32. Paris, 2010.

Beeston, A. F. L. "The Authorship of the Adulis Throne." *BSOAS* 43 (1980): 453–58.

Beeston, A. F. L. "The Chain of al Mandab." In *On Both Sides of al Mandab: Ethiopian, South Arabic and Islamic Studies Presented to Oscar Löfgren on His 90th Birthday*. Stockholm: Svenska Forskningsinstitutet i Istanbul, 1989, 1–6.

Beeston, A. F. L. "The Martyrdom of Azqir." *Proc. Seminar for Arabian Studies* 16 (1985): 5–10. Reprinted in *A. F. L. Beeston at The Arabian Seminar and Other Papers*, ed. M. C. A. Macdonald and C. S. Philips. Oxford: Archaeopress, 2005, 113–18.

Belfiore, Stefano, ed. *Il Geografo e l'Editore: Marciano di Eraclea e I Peripli Antichi*. Rome: Aracne, 2011.

Bezold, Carl. *Kebra Nagast: Die Herrlichkeit der Könige*. Abhandlungen der I Klasse. der Kön. Akad. d. Wissensch. 23, Bd. I. Munich, 1905.

Bowersock, G. W. *Fiction as History, Nero to Julian*. Berkeley: University of California Press, 1994.

Bowersock, G. W. "The Syriac Life of Rabbula and Syrian Hellenism." In *Greek Biography and Panegyric in Late Antiquity*, ed. Tomas Hägg and Philip Rousseau, 255–71. Berkeley: University of California Press, 2000.

Bowersock, G. W. "The New Greek Inscription from South Yemen." In *Qāni' Le port antique du Ḥaḍramawt entre la Méditerranée, l'Afrique et l'Inde*. Preliminary Reports of the Russian Archaeological Mission to the Republic of Yemen, vol. IV, 393–96. Brepols, Belgium: Turnhout, 2010.

Bowersock, G. W. "Helena's Bridle, Ethiopian Christianity, and Syriac Apocalyptic." *Studia Patristica* 45 (2010): 211–20.

Bowersock, G. W. *Empires in Collision in Late Antiquity*. Menahem Stern Jerusalem Lectures. Hanover, NH: Brandeis University Press, 2012.

Bowersock, G. W. "Nonnosus and Byzantine Diplomacy in Arabia." *Rivista Storica Italiana* 124 (2012): 282-290.

Bukharin, Mikhail. "Avtorsvo i datirovka nadpisi *Monumentum Adulitanum* II." *Vestnik Drevneii Istorii* 258 (2006): 3–13.

Bukharin, Mikhail. *Peripl Eritreiskogo Morya*. St. Petersburg: Aleteiya, 2007.

Bukharin, Mikhail. "First Indian Inscription from South Arabia." In *Qāni' Le port antique du Ḥaḍramawt*, ed. J.-F. Salles and A. Sedov, 399–401. Brepols, Belgium: Turnhout, 2010.

Bukharin, Mikhail. "The Notion τὸ πέρας τῆς ἀνακομιδῆς and the Location of Ptolemaïs of the Hunts in the *Periplus of the Erythraean Sea*." *Arabian Archaeology and Epigraphy* 22 (2011): 219–31.

Burstein, Stanley. "Elephants for Ptolemy II: Ptolemaic Policy in Nubia in the Third Century BC." In *Ptolemy II Philadelphus and his World*, ed. P. McKechnie and P. Guillaume. *Mnemosyne* Supplement 300 (Leiden, 2008): 135–147.

Casson, Lionel. *The Periplus Maris Erythaei*. Princeton, NJ: Princeton University Press, 1989.

Casson, Lionel. "Ptolemy II Philadelphus and the Hunting of African Elephants." *TAPA* 123 (1993): 247–60.

Cohen, Getzel M. *The Hellenistic Settlements in Syria, the Red Sea Basin, and North Africa*. Berkeley: University of California Press, 2006.

Conrad, Lawrence. "Abraha and Muḥammad: Some Observations Apropos of Chronology and Literary *topoi* in the Early Arabic Historical Tradition." *BSOAS* 50 (1987): 225–40.

Conti-Rossini, C. "Un documento sul cristianesimo nello Yemen ai tempi del re *Šarāḥbīl* Yakkuf." *Rendiconti dell' Accademia Nazionale dei Lincei, Classe di Scienze morale, storiche e filologiche*, ser. 5, 19 (1910): 705–50.

Crone, Patricia. "The Religion of the Qur'ānic Pagans: God and the Lesser Deities." *Arabica* 57 (2010): 151–200.

Crone, Patricia. "Angels versus Humans as Messengers of God." In *Revelation, Literature, and Community in Late Antiquity*, ed. P. Townsend and M. Vidas, 315–36. Tübingen: Mohr Siebeck, 2011.

Cuvigny, Hélène, and Christian Julien Robin. "Des Kinaidokolpites dans un ostracon grec du désert oriental (Égypte)." *Topoi* 6 (1996): 697–720.

Desanges, Jehan. *Scripta Minora*. Paris: De Boccard, 1999.

Dihle, Albrecht. *Umstrittene Daten*. Cologne: Westdeutscher Verlag, 1965.

Donner, Fred M. *Muhammad and the Believers at the Origins of Islam*. Cambridge, MA: Harvard University Press, 2010.

Fahd, Toufic. *Le Panthéon de l'Arabie centrale à la veille de l'Hégire*. Paris: Paul Geuthner, 1968.

Feissel, Denis. *Chroniques d'épigraphie byzantine*, 1987–2004. Paris: Association des Amis du Centre d'Histoire et Civilisation de Byzance, 2006.

Fiaccadori, Gianfranco. *Teofilo Indiano*. Ravenna: Edizioni del Girasole, 1992.

Fiaccadori, Gianfranco. "Sembrouthes 'Gran Re': Per la storia del primo Ellenismo Aksumita." *La Parola del Passato* 335 (2004): 103–57.

Fiaccadori, Gianfranco. "Gregentios in the Land of the Homerites." In *Life and Works of Saint Gregentios, Archbishop of Taphar*, ed. A. Berger, 48–82. Berlin: De Gruyter, 2006.

Fisher, Greg. *Between Empires: Arabs, Romans, and Sasanians in Late Antiquity*. Oxford: Oxford University Press, 2011.

Fontanella, Francesca. *Elio Aristide: A Roma, traduzione e commento*. Pisa: Edizioni della Normale 2007.

Gajda, Iwona. *Le royaume de Ḥimyar à l'époque monothéiste.* Paris, 2009.

Gawlikowski, Michel. "Odainat et Hérodien, rois des rois." *Mélanges de l'Université St. Joseph* 60 (2007): 289–311.

Hatke, George. *Africans in Arabia Felix: Axumite Relations with Ḥimyar in the Sixth Century* C.E. Ph.D. dissertation [unpublished], Princeton University, January 2011.

Hauben, H. "L'expédition de Ptolémée III en Orient et la sédition domestique de 245 av: J.-C." *Archiv für Papyrologie* 36 (1990): 29–37.

Hawting, Gerald R. *The Idea of Idolatry and the Emergence of Islam: From Polemic to History.* Cambridge: Cambridge University Press, 1999.

Hopkins, Keith. "Brother-Sister Marriage in Roman Egypt." *Comparative Studies in Society and History* 22 (1980): 303–54.

Holland, Tom. *In the Shadow of the Sword.* London: Little, Brown, 2012.

Huebner, Sabine R. "Brother-Sister Marriage in Roman Egypt: A Curiosity of Humankind or a Widespread Family Strategy?" *JRS* 97 (2007): 21–49.

Littmann, Enno. "Adule oder Adulis." In Pauly-Wissowa, *Realencyclopädie: Supplementband* 7 (1940): cols. 1–2.

Macdonald, M. C. A. *The Development of Arabic as a Written Language.* Proceedings of the Seminar for Arabian Studies 40. Oxford, 2010.

Mayerson, Philip. "The Island of Iotabê in the Byzantine Sources: A Reprise." *BASOR* 287 (1992): 1–4.

Millar, Fergus. "Rome's Arab Allies in Late Antiquity. Conceptions and Representations from within the Frontiers of the Empire." In *Commutatio et contentio. Studies in the Late Roman, Sasanian, and Early Islamic Near East in Memory of Zeev Rubin*, ed. H. Börm and J. Wiesehofer, 199–226. Düsseldorf: Wellem Verlag 2010.

Moberg, Axel. *The Book of the Ḥimyarites.* Lund, Sweden: C.W.K. Gleerup, 1924.

Munro-Hay, Stuart. "A New Gold Coin of King MḤDYS of Aksum." *Numismatic Chronicle* 155 (1995): 275–77.

Muravyov, Alexei. "Pervaya volna khristianizatsii." *Vestnik Drevneii Istorii* 261 (2009): 182–85.

Nebe, G. W., and A. Sima. "Die aramäisch / hebräisch / sabäische Grabinschrift der Lea." *Arabian Archaeology and Epigraphy* 15 (2004): 76–83.

Noeldeke, Theodor. *Geschichte der Perser und Araber zur Zeit der Sasaniden, aus der arabischen Chronik des Tabari.* Leiden: Brill, 1879.

Oeconomos, L. "Remarques sur trois passages de trois historiens grecs du Moyen Age." *Byzantion* 20 (1950): 177–83.

Peacock, David, with Lucy Blue and Darren Glazier. *The Ancient Red Sea Port of Adulis, Eritrea: Results of the Eritro-British Expedition, 2004–2005.* Oxford: Oxbow Books, 2007.

Power, Timothy. *The Red Sea from Byzantium to the Caliphate* AD 500–1000. Cairo: American University of Cairo Press, 2012.

Robin, Christian Julien. "La première intervention abyssine en Arabie méridionale." *Proceedings of the Eighth International Conference of Ethiopian Studies*, 157–62. Addis Ababa: Institute of Ethiopian Studies, 1989.

Robin, Christian Julien. "Ḥimyar et Israël." *CRAI* (2004): 831–908.

Robin, Christian Julien. "Les Arabes de Ḥimyar, 'des Romains' et des Perses (IIIe—VIe siècles de l'ère chrétienne)." *Semitica et Classica* 1 (2008): 167–202.

Robin, Christian Julien. "Joseph, dernier roi de Ḥimyar (de 522 à 525, ou une des années suivantes)." *Jerusalem Studies in Arabic and Islam* 34 (2008): 1–124.

Robin, Christian Julien, and Maria Gorea. "Les vestiges antiques de la grotte de Ḥôq (Suqutra, Yémen)." *CRAI* (2002): 409–45.

Roller, Duane W. *The World of Juba II and Kleopatra Selene*. London: Routledge, 2003.

Rubin, Uri. "Ḥanīfiyya and Ka'ba." *Jerusalem Studies in Arabic and Islam* 13 (1990): 85–112.

Ryckmans, Jacques. "Inscriptions historiques sabéennes de l'Arabie centrale: Inscription de Muraighān." *Le Muséon* 56 (1953): 339–42.

Scullard, H. H. *The Elephant in the Greek and Roman World*. London: Thames and Hudson, 1974.

Shahîd (Kawar), Irfān. "Byzantium and Kinda." *Byzantinische Zeitschrift* 53 (1960): 57–73.

Shahîd (Kawar), Irfān. *The Martyrs of Najrân: New Documents*. Brussels: Société des Bollandistes, 1971.

Shahîd (Kawar), Irfān. "Byzantium in South Arabia." *Dumbarton Oaks Papers* 33 (1979): 25–94.

Speck, Bert van der, and Irving Finkel. Babylonian Chronicle website: http://www.livius.org/cg-cm/chronicles/bchp-ptolemy_iii/bchp_ptolemy_iii_02.html.

Taylor, David G. K. "A Stylistic Comparison of the Syriac Ḥimyarite Martyr Texts Attributed to Simeon of Beth Arsham." In *Juifs et Chrétiens en Arabie*, ed. Joëlle Beaucamp, Françoise Briquel-Chatonnet, and Christian Julien Robin, 143–76.

Villeneuve, François. "Une inscription latine sur l'archipel Farasân, Arabie Séoudite, sud de la mer Rouge." *CRAI* (2004): 419–29.

Villeneuve, François, with C. Phillips and W. Facey. "Une inscription latine de l'archipel Farasân (sud de la mer Rouge) et son contexte archéologique et historique." *Arabia* 2 (2004): 143–90, with figs. 63–67.

Wolska-Conus, Wanda. *La topographie chrétienne de Cosmas Indicopleustes: Théologie et sciences au VIe siècle*. Paris: Presses Universitaires de France, 1962.

Yule, Paul. *Ḥimyar. Spätantike im Jemen/Late Antique Yemen*. Aichwald: Linden Soft 2007.

Index

Note: Page numbers in *italics* refer to illustrations.

Ella Asbeha. *See* Kālēb
Eritrea, 6, 7, 10, 31
Esimphaios (Sumyafa Ashwaʿ), 103, 106, 111
Ethiopia
Byzantium alliance with, 4, 107, 117, 121, 142, 157n2, 162n25
capital city of, 7 (*see also* Axum)
Christianity in, 65, 66–67, 74–75, 81–83
coinage of, 61, 64, 75–76, *101*
commercial interests of, 157n2
and Egypt, 43, 52–53
elephants of, 35–37, 39
expulsion of Ethiopians from Arabia, 117–118
Geʿez script of, 14, 32, 69–70
and Gulf of Zula, 7
Ḥimyar campaign (518), 93, 94, 95
Ḥimyar campaign (525), 4–5, 21, 25, 91, 92, 97–98, 103, 106
Ḥimyar occupation (third century), 45, 55–56, 59, 60, 61, 63–64, 78–79
imperialism of, 5, 14, 25, 48, 63
and Jews, 82
Justin's calls for intervention, 5, 96–97, 156n6
and "king of kings" phrase, 64–65
languages used in, 32
map of, *xxii*
and Meroitic kingdom, 43
Monophysite Christianity in, 121
Muslim Believers' immigration to, 123–126
and Nubia, 53–54
power of rulers, 33, 120–121
and regional power shifts, 120–123
royal line of, 82, 87
as Solomon's descendants, 81–82, 87, 102
sovereignty claims of, 14, 61–62, 64
term, 53–54
and Zoskales, 31
Euphrasius, 138

Fragmenta Historicorum Graecorum (Müller), 136
Frumentius, 66–67, 75

Gabaz, Ella, 12
Gabaza (harbor of Adulis), 12, 97
Gadara, 55–56, 57, 58, 78
Gaius Caesar, 27
Gajda, Iwona, 87
Gaza, *xxii*
Geography (Ptolemy) 56
Getae, 54
Greek language, 26–27, 31–32, 45
Gregentius 103, 104
Gulf of Aqaba, 108
Gulf of Zula
as access point to Adulis and Axum, 12
history of name, 7
and location of Adulis Throne, *13*
Pliny the Elder on, 27

Habab, 50
Haddas river, 9
Ḥaḍramawt, 63, 80
ḥanīf references, 127–129, 130
Ḥārith ibn Jabala, 111, 114

Hawting, Gerald, 126–127, 130, 159n15
Ḥayyān, 95
Hebrew Bible, 131
Hebrews, Epistle to, 29
Heliodorus, 60
The Hellespont, 40, 42
Heracles, 38, 149n4
Heraclius, 125
Hermes, 38, 131, 149n4
Herodotus, 39, 53
Ḥimyar kingdom
  Byzantium support of, 121
  Christian kingdom installed in, 5, 93, 94–95, 103, 105
  Christian persecution in, 3, 76, 85–91, 92
  churches in, 103–104, 114
  dissolution of, 117
  emergence of, 63–64
  Ethiopian campaign against (518), 93, 94, 95
  Ethiopian campaign against (525), 4–5, 21, 25, 91, 92, 97–98, 103, 106
  Ethiopian occupation of (third century), 45, 55–56, 59, 60, 61, 63–64, 78–79
  Ethiopian sovereignty claims, 14, 61–62, 64, 79, 95
  expulsion of Ethiopians from Arabia, 117–118
  Judaism in, 3–4, 5, 80, 83–86, 93–94
  Kālēb's shrine built in, 95–96
  kings of, 79 (*see also* Abraha; Yūsuf As'ar Yath'ar)
  location of, *xxii*
  Persian control of, 120
  and Ramla conference, 89–90
  social and political upheavals in, 76
  titulature in, 79, 83
Hippolytus, 56
al-Hīra, *xxii*, 114
Hubal (pagan deity), 5, 86, 116, 126

Ibn al-Mujāwir, 98
Ibn Khaldun, 53
India, 23
Iotabê, Jewish settlement on, 108
Islam
  and Abraham (biblical), 127–130
  Arabia as crucible of, 87
  emigrations of Believers, 123–126
  ḥanīf references in, 127–129, 130
  and idolatry, 126–127, 128
  and Jerusalem, 6
  and monotheism, 127–131, 159n15
  Muḥammad's emigration (*hijra*) to Medina, xix, 115, 118, 125–126, 133
  and paganism, 126–127, 130
  Qur'ān, 116, 123, 126–127, 130, 159n15
  rise of, 6, 119, 122
ivory trade, 31, 39, 42

Jerusalem, *xxii*
  Byzantine hegemony in, 122
  Church of the Holy Sepulchre, 122
  and Islam, 6
  Persia's capture of (614), 5–6, 118, 122–123
  Vespasian's devastation of, 80